Library of
Davidson College

Charles Darwin in Western Australia

A Young Scientist's Perception of an Environment

PATRICK ARMSTRONG

UNIVERSITY OF WESTERN AUSTRALIA PRESS, NEDLANDS, W.A.

Western Australian Experience Series

*First published in 1985
by University of Western Australia Press
Nedlands, Western Australia 6009*

Agents: Eastern States of Australia, New Zealand and Papua New Guinea: Melbourne University Press, Carlton South, Vic. 3053; U.K., Europe, Africa and Middle East: Peter Moore, P.O. Box 66, 200a Perne Road, Cambridge CB1 3PD, England; U.S.A., Canada and the Caribbean: International Specialized Book Services Inc., P.O. Box 1632, Beaverton, Oregon 97075 U.S.A.

This book is copyright. Apart from any fair dealing for the purposes of private study, research, criticism or review, as permitted under the Copyright Act, no part may be reproduced by any process without written permission. Enquiries should be made to the publisher.

© Patrick Armstrong 1985

National Library of Australia Cataloguing-in-Publication data

Armstrong, Patrick, 1941- .
  Charles Darwin in Western Australia.

  Includes index.
  ISBN 0 85564 237 8.

  1. Darwin, Charles, 1809-1882 — Journeys —
  Western Australia. 2. Darwin, Charles, 1809-1882 —
  Views on Western Australia. 3. Natural history —
  Western Australia. 4. Western Australia —
  Description and travel — To 1850. I. Title. (Series:
  Western Australian experience series).

574.9941

  ISSN 0815—9513 = *Western Australian experience series.*

Photoset by the University of Western Australia Press; printed by Frank Daniels Pty Ltd, Perth; and bound by Printers Trade Services, Belmont.

To the memory of my father
EDWARD ARMSTRONG (1900–1978)
A Parson Naturalist

Foreword

'Not another account of that man and that voyage' I can almost hear some say. This is, however, not just another account but an unearthing of new and a sifting of old facts pertinent to the only scientific theory which changed people's idea of themselves.

This delightful essay also gives new insight into Western Australia as it was before it was hit by 'northern culture' and of Darwin himself and the culture from which he came.

The references and speculation concerning Darwin's Red Book are of great interest and must be viewed within the timespan of the development of the theory of evolution.

Darwin visited Western Australia thirty-five years after the French naturalist Francois Peron, whose accounts contain much which senses the transmutability of species.

The Red Book predates Alfred Russel Wallace's first publication which states 'Every species has come into existence coincident both in space and time with pre-existing closely allied species' by some eighteen years. Wallace came to his conclusions while working on the flora and fauna of the archipelago to the north of Australia.

This essay suggests that Darwin's Little Red Book might have originated out of his brief encounter with the natural history of Western Australia. Whether this is true or not, Darwin's visit to this corner of the great island continent is an important link in the chain of events which allowed the world a better understanding of itself.

I hope that every Australian will take note of this work of scholarship and strive to ensure that not more of the natural heritage of their enormous slice of real estate need find its way into that ever growing Red Data Book, which lists the world's endangered species.

David Bellamy
Bedburn
Co. Durham
England
1985

Contents

	Page
Foreword	vi
Acknowledgements	viii
A Note on Circumstances	1
Introduction	3
CHAPTER 1: The Sources, and Their Relationships to Published Work: Darwin's Method of Working	6
CHAPTER 2: The Chronology and Topography of the *Beagle*'s Visit to Western Australia	13
CHAPTER 3: Darwin's Perception of the West Australian Environment	30
CHAPTER 4: Geological Investigations	41
CHAPTER 5: The Effect of the Visit on Darwin's Development: (i) The Evolution of a Model of a Changing World	51
CHAPTER 6: The Effect of the Visit on Darwin's Development: (ii) Strange Beings of an Isolated Continent	59
Appendix: Australia, the *Red Notebook* and the Transmutation Theory	67
Notes	73

Acknowledgements

IT IS A PLEASURE and a privilege to acknowledge the assistance of the many individuals and organisations who have assisted in the preparation of this work.

I thank particularly the Master and Fellows of Darwin College, Cambridge, who afforded me the ideal environment for the preparation of the first draft of this work by the granting of a Visiting Associateship during 1982-83. My best thanks to Dr Harold Whitehouse who suggested I apply for the Associateship. I thank also Mr Peter Gautrey, curator of the Cambridge University Library Manuscripts Collection, and an authority on the Darwin Archives, and other staff at the library: the library also supplied photographs of some manuscripts (Figs 7, 9, 10, 12, 13 and 14).

My debt to previous students of Darwin's work will be only too clear from the list of notes and references. I would mention Howard Gruber's *Darwin on Man*, and Sandra Herbert's introduction to *The Red Note Book of Charles Darwin* as publications I found particularly useful.

To Dr Bob Keenan of Pace University, New York, I am indebted for a number of stimulating conversations on matters Darwinian during a Cambridge autumn, and for most detailed and careful comment on an early draft. Professor Geoff Martin of Southern Connecticut State University encouraged me to persist with the study of Darwin's influence, besides helping me to get through a certain quantity of wine and cheese in Paris.

My employer, the University of Western Australia, granted me leave of absence to visit Cambridge in 1982-83, and financially supported fieldwork in Western Australia.

Mr David Murray, Head of the Department of Geography (1982-1985), provided endless encouragement for the project besides commenting very carefully on the text. Many members of the technical and secretarial staff assisted: Miss Sally Higgs did the word-processing, Mrs Michelle Bekle (née Ley) drew the diagrams and Mr Roger Webber undertook the photographic work.

Finally I am most deeply grateful to my former teacher, Prof. David Bellamy, for agreeing to write the foreword.

I thank them all.

A Note on Circumstances

I SUPPOSE THAT MY INTEREST IN, and curiosity concerning, the Darwin Family can be traced to the times when, as a young child in Cambridge, I used to see artist Gwen Raverat (1885-1957), one of Charles Darwin's brilliant grandchildren, with her easel. She was already, by then, an elderly lady, but I have the most vivid recollections of her, in a wheelchair, painting along the Backs, around Newnham Mill, or on Laundress Green. Later I read her *Period Piece* about her childhood and adolescence in the Cambridge of the 1880s and '90s, a book lively with recollections of one of the world's most gifted families, and so it was a great privilege to be able to take up an Associateship at Darwin College in late 1982: the College now occupies the building (Newnham Grange) that was the home of the Darwin family from 1885 to 1962.

The first draft of this essay was therefore written beneath the watchful eyes of both Charles and Emma, as well as those of Charles' great-uncle (William Alvey Darwin, 1726-1783) and great grandmother (Elizabeth Darwin, née Hill, 1702-1797) who grace the walls of Darwin College Library, once the dining room of Newnham Grange. It was written while I was seated at a table that had been owned (between 1932 and 1962) by Sir Charles Darwin (1887-1962, another grandchild of Charles Robert), and that had been made while H.M.S. *Beagle* was on her epoque-making voyage.

There is one further point of contact. When my father, Edward Armstrong, died in Cambridge in 1978, I inherited part of his library: among the books that came to me in this manner was a copy of the Everyman edition of *The Voyage of the Beagle*; the only annotation in the book was a note drawing attention to Charles Darwin's description of the Aboriginal emu dance, witnessed by Charles during his visit to King George's Sound. I turned to the appropriate page and re-read Darwin's description of Western Australia, where I had by then made my own home. His outspokenness made me feel I had to enquire further.

Introduction

THIS STUDY WAS COMMENCED in the belief that it would be mainly of local interest—of concern principally to those who knew the part of Western Australia herein described, and who might feel that the reactions of a great scientist, at an early point in his career, to their environment, were of some consequence. Although the time spent by Charles Darwin in Western Australia was brief—just over a week—it nevertheless did appear to be surprisingly little documented: R. D. Keynes' encyclopaedic *The Beagle Record* (1979) barely mentions the visit to King George's Sound, and A. J. Marshall's *Darwin and Huxley in Australia* (published in 1970, but written over two decades earlier) devotes only ten lines to this part of Darwin's itinerary; Mea Allan's beautiful *Darwin and His Flowers* (1977) simply mentions his brief description of grass trees.

However, in due course there appeared grounds for believing that Darwin's experience in Australia, including Western Australia, was of some significance in the shaping of his *weltanschauung* or 'view of the world', that eventually manifests itself in his writing of the revolutionary works, *Origin of Species* (1859) and *Descent of Man* (1871).

This account, therefore, has several objectives: to provide, as far as it can be reconstructed, a factual description of Charles Darwin's visit to Western Australia; to examine the way in which he observed the West Australian environment and the manner in which he recorded it; and to consider what effect the visit had upon him, both at the time, and subsequently.

But before we disembark with Charles Robert Darwin from the ten-gun brig H.M.S. *Beagle* at King George the Third Sound, on the fine, breezy morning of 7 March 1836, we may perhaps with advantage, briefly review the previous twenty-six-and-a-half years of his life.

Born into a successful Shropshire doctor's family in 1809, he was admitted to Shrewsbury School in 1818. He entered the same year as Charles Wicksteed, a member of what was to become an important antipodean family, and a year ahead of B. H. Kennedy, who became one of the foremost classical scholars of his generation. He was at the school during the headmastership (1798-1836) of the Reverend Samuel Butler, D.D., and his contemporaries, for the most part, went on to become country clergy, to serve as army or naval officers (some of them with great distinction), or to the law.[1] He left school not altogether unwillingly, in 1825, and was sent to study medicine in Edinburgh for two years. The venture was not a success, and in 1828 he entered Christ's College, Cambridge, with the vague thought of becoming a country parson: he took his B.A. in 1831. His academic career at Cambridge was not a great deal more propitious than his days at Shrewsbury or in Edinburgh, but it gave him an opportunity to extend his schoolboy hobby, natural history, and, particularly, to develop his friendship with the Reverend Professor John Stevens Henslow, Professor of Botany, accompanying him on numerous excursions into the East Anglian countryside. Indeed, Charles Darwin became known as 'he who walks with Henslow'.[2] He also formed an acquaintance with Adam Sedgwick, Professor of Geology at Cambridge from 1818 to 1873, and in the summer of 1831 he went on a geological excursion through North Wales with him. These two associations, and the interests developed through them, were to prove of enormous importance.

As the result of Professor Henslow's connections, on his return to Shrewsbury from the North Wales trip in late August, 1831, he received the offer of the appointment as Naturalist on the *Beagle* expedition. He accepted the position only after considerable opposition from his father: it was Charles' uncle (and eventual father-in-law), Josiah Wedgwood, who persuaded Dr Darwin to allow his twenty-two-year-old son to accept the position, and the ship sailed, after a couple of false starts due to bad weather, late in December 1831.

The *Beagle* visited the Cape Verde Islands and St Paul's Rocks (February 1832), and many parts of South America (1832-1835), the Falkland Islands (1833 and again in 1834) before the much discussed sojourn in the Galapagos (September-October 1835) and the crossing of the Pacific to Tahiti (November 1835) and New Zealand (December). Darwin arrived in Port Jackson, New South Wales on 12 January 1836, and journeyed to Bathurst before returning to the coast and crossing to Hobart Town in Van Diemen's Land. He stayed in Tasmania from 5 to 17 February 1836, the day the *Beagle* commenced her crossing of the Great Australian Bight, prior to her arrival in King George's Sound, the site of the first British settlement in Western Australia (founded 1826), on the south coast of the state (Fig. 1).

Throughout his travels Charles collected and observed: he collected tens of thousands of specimens[3] of plants, insects, reptiles, mammals, molluscs, birds, rocks, fossils and minerals, and covered several thousand pages of manuscript with descriptions of the various environments he encountered. These manuscripts, remarkably well written, comprised principally the *Diary of Observations on Zoology of the Places visited during the Voyage*, and the *Diary on the Geology of the Places visited during the Voyage*, together with associated notes;[4] they formed the basis for a very great deal of Charles' subsequent work.

Figure 1—The Settlement King George's Sound by Isaac Scott Nind c. 1829. (Photograph: The Art Gallery of Western Australia)

Chapter 1

THE SOURCES AND THEIR RELATIONSHIPS TO PUBLISHED WORK: DARWIN'S METHOD OF WORKING

THROUGHOUT MUCH OF HIS JOURNEYING, the young Darwin recorded his field observations in small, leather-bound note-books. There are some eighteen of these, and they contain personal memoranda on practical matters—such as shopping lists of items to be purchased at ports of call—as well as scientific observations.[5] There are no entries in these books for New Zealand, Van Diemen's Land or King George's Sound, and Nora Barlow (yet another of Charles' granddaughters) in *Charles Darwin and the Beagle* (John Murray, London, 1946) assumed that the notebooks containing his observations on these places had been lost. I believe, however, that they may never have existed, for certainly in Tasmania and Western Australia, Charles excursions were more in the nature of 'day trips' rather than extended explorations, and so it is quite possible that he was able to write up his observations regularly in his cabin on the *Beagle*, and was less dependant on the *aide memoire* provided by his pencilled notebook jottings. A very rough draft of a description of the geology of the King George's Sound area is to be found in the Darwin Archives in Cambridge.[6] Also, this document has, on its reverse, further pencilled memoranda concerning the geology of the area, similar in character to those made in the notebooks in other places; these jottings have some appearance of being made in the field.[7]

Charles' normal procedure was to write up his notes into a more formally complete form when he had a little leisure, probably in his cabin on H.M.S. *Beagle* while the ship was sailing from one port to another. He often combined his observations and speculations with those of earlier explorers and other scientists, for, contrary to what is sometimes supposed, Darwin and Captain FitzRoy (Fig. 2), Commander of the *Beagle*, with whom he shared a cabin, had at their disposal a substantial library of reference works, and this was to some extent kept up to date throughout the voyage.[8]

In addition to the *Geological* and *Zoological Diaries*, Charles kept a more personal *Journal*; this, as well as including descriptions of scientific phenomena from the *Diaries*, contained material of more direct human interest. The *Journal* formed the basis of Charles Darwin's most popular

Figure 2—Captain FitzRoy Commander of H.M.S. *Beagle*, 1831-1836. (Photograph: Mitchell Library, Sydney)

work, *The Voyage of the Beagle*,[9] but the published version is considerably altered from the original manuscript. For example, additional material from the *Geological* and *Zoological Diaries*, the comments of scientific colleagues and additional references were included, while amongst the deletions is an account of the European settlement at King George's Sound.[10] The style is also improved. In his description of the geological development of the Bald Head fossiliferous site (see pp. 46 and 47) the *Journal*'s rendering:

> The weather is now again in parts wearing away these soft rocks and hence the harder casts of the roots and branches stand out in exact imitation of a dead shrubbery

becomes, in the published *Voyage*,

> The weather is now wearing away the softer parts, and in consequence the hard casts of the roots and branches of the trees project above the surface, and, in a singularly deceptive manner, resemble the stumps of a dead thicket.

His writing is generally quite legible, although the modern eye has difficulty with the occasional word: he seems sometimes to have written at considerable speed. His spelling is not altogether consistent (dike and dyke, colour and color, Sidney and Sydney occur), and he frequently uses the long '∫' where 'double s' occurs. His punctuation and use of capital letters sometimes appear fairly arbitrary. And although the meaning of his prose is almost invariably clear, his style is occasionally convoluted, and words are sometimes left out. In a few places ink-spills mar the manuscript – the result of stormy weather giving the *Beagle* a rough passage perhaps. Charles didn't always give the full date, and, very rarely, he appears to be in error: a page of his notes on the Cocos-Keeling Islands is dated 1835, yet in fact he visited that archipelago in April 1836, *after* having visited Western Australia. (Figs 7, 9, 10 and 12 show selected pages from the *Beagle* diaries, and Fig. 3 shows some of the relationships between the various Darwinian sources dating from the *Beagle* period.)

Other important records compiled during the voyage, include lists of specimens, sometimes very fully annotated. The following from Darwin's *List of Shells*[11] provides an example:

1836 King George's Sound   March.

3560   Bulimus (2 species) from calcareous sand hills at Bald Head: and a Physa, freshwater lake: King George's Sound.

3562   Natica, taken off tidal rocks. Being kept by accident in some *dry* paper, *in* my cabin; I found to my astonishment that 12 days afterwards, the animal was still quite alive.

3563   Marine tidal shells.

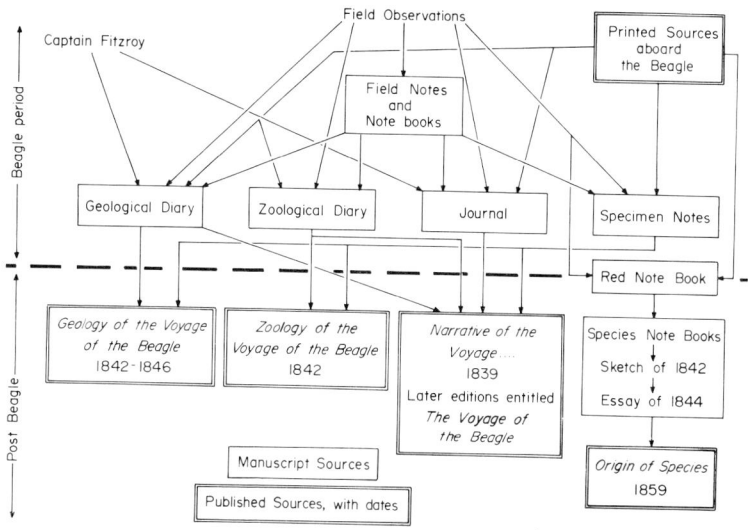

Figure 3—Diagram showing relationships between the various *Beagle* Darwin sources showing the 'flow' of ideas. The upper part of the diagram shows the sources dating from the actual voyage, the lower part is those compiled after the return to England. The *Red Notebook* was commenced aboard the *Beagle* (probably during or just after the visit, to Australia) but continued in England.

Besides shells, we know that Charles collected a large number of fish specimens, many of them 'caught by net in Princess Royal Harbour'.[12] His eye for detail can be seen in his descriptions, such as:

1389 Skate, above muddy cream colour.
1390 Fish, above varied dull green, with pale ditto, beneath snow white.
1391 Fish, pale copperish brown with water marks of a fine darker brown.
1392 Fish, very pale brown, fins pale orange.
1393 Fish, mottled with pale blackish green, leaving white spots.
1394 Fish, sides fine dark green, and pale silvery green, fins tipped with red, Iris fine green, handsome fish.

The fish volume (Part IV) of the *Zoology of the Voyage of the Beagle*[13] edited by the Reverend Leonard Jenyns, includes nine species of fish from King George's Sound.

Darwin also attempted to catch mammals in Western Australia. In the

Mammals volume of the *Zoology of the Voyage*, by George Waterhouse, there is a description of *Mus fusipes*, with the note: 'This animal was caught in a trap baited with cheese, amongst the bushes at King George's Sound.' Darwin discussed the specimen with Waterhouse, and his file contains a note[14] comparing it with an eastern Australian form, and with South American species (see p. 12). He also collected some 25 rock and fossil specimens (petrified tree material, limestones, sandstones, granite and gneiss), some insects, several dozen species of shells,[15] but apparently no plants, birds or reptiles.

Charles was in some ways, quite systematic in his collecting. Amongst his notes from the *Beagle* period is a very detailed set of instructions[16] for the preservation of specimens, apparently compiled from the advice of friends and colleagues in the hurried days before the *Beagle* sailed. Professor Henslow, for example, seems to have urged the young collector to 'Lay seeds in the capsule in brown paper' and to keep them 'dry but not hot'. Darwin was usually quite punctilious about numbering and labelling his specimens.

Some years after the *Beagle* returned, he was asked to contribute to a scientific manual for those going on comparable expeditions,[17] and he wrote:

> Every single specimen ought to be numbered with a printed number (those which can be read upside down having a stop after them), and a book kept exclusively for their entry. As the value of many specimens depends entirely on the stratum or locality whence they were procured being known it is highly necessary that every specimen should be ticketed on the same day when collected. If this be not done, in after years, the collector cannot be sure that his tickets and references are correct . . .

The voice of experience seem to be speaking here; occasionally in the piles of notes one encounters an annotation of uncertainty, or a question mark, that hints of the frustration of the mature scientist at his own youthful lapses.[18] On the whole, however, Darwin practised what he preached.

We know that he was well equipped for his mission: the geological hammer he used, along with some of his dissecting instruments, and a sample of the type of specimen-box he used may be inspected today at Down House (see footnote 5). He also had a microscope, and the cabin that he shared with Captain FitzRoy was stuffed with books: his copy of the first edition of Lyell's *Principles of Geology*, now preserved in Cambridge, is falling to pieces with use, much of it probably during the voyage of H.M.S. *Beagle*. He also had the writings of Humboldt and King. Captain FitzRoy had with him a copy of Flinders' *Voyage to Terra Australis*, and made use of it frequently: in his *Narrative* FitzRoy records his debt to the pioneer hydrographer from Lincolnshire:

Before quitting King George's Sound I must add my slight testimony to the skill and accuracy with which Flinders laid down and described New Holland and Van Diemen's Land ... His accounts also of wind, weather, climate, currents and tides, are excellent.

Darwin makes reference to all these sources, and also the writings of French explorer-authors such as Labillardière, in his *Geological and Zoological Diaries*. Interestingly the final page of the Red Notebook (CUL/DAR unclassified, see Appendix) contains a table for converting French metric to imperial units.

Although later in his life Charles was in the habit of covering his books with annotations, he does not seem to have done this to the same extent while aboard the *Beagle*: a pity.

We may picture, then, the young Charles Darwin, as he goes about his work. By day he is striding purposefully through the bush and scrub of southwestern Australia or clambering over the rocks along the shores of King George's Sound, hammer at his belt, notes in hand. In the evening we see him writing up his diaries by the light of a lantern, seated at the chart table in his tiny cabin; the table is cluttered with his microscope, numerous rock specimens and several open books; the timbers of the *Beagle* groan a little from time to time as the ship shifts while she lies at anchor a couple of cable's lengths out from the tiny settlement clinging to the shore of the Sound.

The specimens he collected during the voyage were sent back, at convenient intervals, to his friend and former teacher, Professor Henslow in Cambridge (although it is fair to assume that the Australian specimens accompanied Darwin on the *Beagle* — alternative arrangements would not have led to their arrival in England any more quickly). Naturally Darwin's first obligation when the ship docked at Falmouth in October 1836 was to journey to Shrewsbury to visit his family, but within three weeks there began a period of several months' intensive work in London and Cambridge. This involved the sorting of his collections, writing up the scientific results of the voyage,[19] and, we now know, the early stages of the development in his mind of the theory of the 'transmutability of species'. It seems probable his experiences in Australia (taken of course, with his recollections of South America, the Galapagos and the other varied locales of his explorations) constituted a significant influence upon him in this phrenetic period of sorting, thinking, writing and discussion of his work with the leading English scientists of his day. He corresponded with Charles Babington, the Cambridge entomologist, and F. W. Hope, another distinguished entomologist about the distinctiveness of Australian insects; Darwin was always eager to compare his own specimens, descriptions and ideas with those of others.

The following letter[20] was included amongst Charles' own notes on the *Beagle* specimens:

St John's Coll, Cambridge
July 1 1837

Dear Darwin,
I returned here yesterday evening & found your letter lying upon my table. Will you tell Hope that I have only one insect from Australia that is King George's Sound. It is a Hydroporus allied to 12-punctata, but smaller and less marked with yellow. I will complete a description of it during the following week and send it to you for Hope . . .

Charles C. Babington.

The note below[21] probably dates from this time and typifies Charles' interest both in the uniqueness of Australia's fauna, and its relationship with that of the other land masses:

Mr. Waterhouse has two mice from Australia which are very unlike each other (one is mine from King George's Sound) yet they both [?illegible] resemble in general form the South American species and this form is distinct from those of the whole of the rest of the world. — Mr. Waterhouse showed me [a] small animal [?illegible] brought from Australia with very close resemblance to *Phila Didiphila* — Marsupial continent . . How is it with reptiles . . .?

The significance of this period of frantic activity — sorting, writing, thinking and discussion — on Charles Darwin's intellectual development, and the importance of his recollections of his Australian experiences within it, will be returned to later.

There is one further source that we may, in due course, consider in our search for Charles' observations on Western Australia (and other parts of the continent): his letters. Throughout his life he was a prodigious correspondent, and his time on the *Beagle* was no exception. Particularly interesting are those to his sisters, of whom he seems to have been extremely fond, and his friendly mentor, Professor Henslow. Fortunately most of these have been preserved, and some indeed published.[22]

Chapter 2

THE CHRONOLOGY AND TOPOGRAPHY OF THE *Beagle*'s VISIT TO WESTERN AUSTRALIA

CHARLES DARWIN'S ACCOUNT of the eight days spent at King George's Sound, Western Australia, as recorded in the *Voyage* is extremely short — just two pages. Yet the brief description is remarkably all-embracing: in it he makes mention of the rocks, landforms, soil, plants, animals, Aborigines and the weather. The original *Journal* version had a very brief account of the European settlement, but this was excised from the 1839 publication of the *Voyage*. Darwin's published descriptions of the Sound are excellently complemented by Captain FitzRoy's annotations on the locality.[23] The latter are of course written in the style of the naval man that FitzRoy was, rather than that of a scientist, but they are valuable in that they in some instances provide information on matters upon which Darwin is silent. For example, included in the Captain's *Narrative* are detailed meteorological observations.

Captain FitzRoy's 'official' account also provided a transcript of the instructions he was given on the sailing of the *Beagle* from Plymouth. The surveys to be conducted were spelt out therein in great detail: accuracy was not to be sacrificed, the heights of headlands were to be determined by angular measurement, magnetic observations were to be made, distances were to be accurately determined. Despite the surveys of King and Flinders of the decades before the *Beagle*'s sailing, much of the southern hemisphere remained relatively unexplored, and there was, in Britain, a real hunger for accurate hydrographic charts, and for scientific and economic intelligence, both for naval purposes and the expansion of trade.

That part of the Admiralty's instructions that deals with Australia and the Indian Ocean[24] is perhaps worth quoting in full:

> From Port Jackson her course [i.e. that of the *Beagle*] will depend upon the time of year. If it be made by the southward, she might touch at Hobart Town, King George's Sound, and Swan River, to determine the difference in longitude from thence to Mauritius ...
>
> If she should have to quit Port Jackson about the middle of the year, her passage must be through Torres Strait ... And perhaps, in crossing the ocean, if circumstances are favourable, she might look at the Keeling Islands and settle their position ...

The *Beagle* in fact sailed from Port Jackson on 30 January 1836, at the height of the southern hemisphere summer, and thus, quite correctly, Captain FitzRoy took the southerly route. However, the actual course taken by the ship was something of a compromise, for the Swan River was not visited (what would Darwin's comments have been upon Perth and Fremantle, I wonder?), yet the *Beagle* did put in to the Cocos-Keeling Islands. Darwin's ideas on coral reefs and atolls were just developing, and a first draft of his paper on this subject had been written in about December 1835,[25] and his theory was confirmed at Keeling. As Charles shared the Captain's cabin, it is tempting to believe that the Ship's Naturalist's enthusiasm was, at least marginally, a factor in Captain FitzRoy's decision to deviate from the direct east-west, Western Australia to Mauritius route, at the cost of a call at Swan River.

Darwin records, in the *Voyage*, the passage from Hobart Town and the arrival in Western Australia with great economy:

> February 17.[26] — The *Beagle* sailed from Tasmania, and on the 6th of the ensuing month, reached King George's Sound, situated close to the S.W. corner of Australia. We staid there eight days . . .

The original *Journal* entry, however, while hardly verbose, does allow us to learn a little more about conditions en route:

> [February] 17th. The *Beagle* stood out with a fair wind on her passage to King George's Sound. The Gun-room officers gave a passage to England to Mr Duff of the 21st Regiment.
>
> March 6th. In the evening came to an anchor in the mouth of the inner harbor of King George's Sound. Our passage has been a tolerable one; & what is surprising we had not a single encounter with a gale of wind. Yet to me, from that long Westerly swell, the time has passed with no little misery. We staid there eight days . . .

FitzRoy's account confirms this description in almost every detail: his meteorological record shows that winds were generally of Force 4 or below, but often had a westerly component; there were blue skies and light clouds (although on 19 February a southerly wind reached Force 7, the barometer fell to 29.85 inches, and the weather was noted as being overcast, cloudy and misty, with passing showers and squalls). His *Narrative* reads:

> On the 17th we sailed out of the picturesque Derwent, an arm of the sea extending inland many miles beyond Hobart Town, and thence worked our way southward around the land of Van Diemen. We then steered westwards, or as much so as contrary winds would admit, until we made land off King George's Sound on 6th March; and a few hours afterwards moored at the principal anchorage called Princess Royal Harbour; a wide but shallow place, with a very narrow entrance.[27]

Captain FitzRoy goes on to give a brief, somewhat critical, account of the landscape as seen from the anchorage, beginning the following paragraph: 'Next day, however, we found that . . .' The meteorological record shows the location of the *Beagle* at 10.00 a.m. on March 6 as 'King George's Sound, the winds "variable" the weather "squally"'. These accounts can be reconciled by assuming that although the ship came within sight of the Sound about mid-morning on the 6th, for some hours progress was slow, and it was late afternoon before the anchor was cast. Neither Darwin nor FitzRoy went ashore that evening.

The next day, Monday March 7, at 10.00 a.m. at least, it was fine, the barometer 30.19 inches and rising, the air temperature 63.5 °F, and some white clouds were being swept across the blue West Australian sky by a fresh breeze (Force 5).

One of the first things that some of the officers of the *Beagle* did on arriving at the Sound was to undertake navigational observations. The statistical appendix to Captain FitzRoy's *Narrative* reveals that these were performed at the 'new Government Buildings, at the east side of Princess Royal Harbour, near the water'. Among other measurements, it was necessary to compare the readings of twenty chronometers (they had been set in Hobart, shortly before the *Beagle* sailed).

It is also recorded that magnetic observations were made by Lt. Bartholomew James Sullivan. While some of the ship's crew were assisting him, Captain FitzRoy and the Ship's Naturalist ventured inland, examining the small settlement and visiting the farm of Sir Richard Spencer:

> Behind a hill, which separates the harbour from the sound, a thick wood was discovered, where there were many trees of considerable size; and in the midst of this wood I found Sir Richard Spencer's house, much resembling a small but comfortable farm-house in England. Immediately around Sir Richard's house a few fields had been cleared and cultivated in the midst of the wood.[28]

FitzRoy goes on to say that 'This sort of isolated residence has a charm for some minds . . .' but makes it quite clear that he could not tolerate the isolation, 'numerous privations', and 'loss of society'.

Charles Darwin's own *Journal* account is more succinct, but very similar:

> At a distance of a mile over the hill, Sir R. Spencer has a small & neat farm, & what is the only cultivated ground in the district.

Captain Sir Richard Spencer, R.N., K.C.H., late of Lyme Regis, Dorset, had arrived to take up the position of Government Resident in Albany in September 1833, after a distinguished naval career during which he had served under Nelson. He purchased the Government Farm at Strawberry Hill at valuation — £206 14s 6d — having brought seeds, stock,

Figure 4—The Old Farm, Strawberry Hill, as it appears today. (Photograph: Patrick Armstrong)

fruit trees and implements from England, along with Welsh slates and other building materials. The dwelling house was, at the time of Darwin and FitzRoy's visit, largely of wattle and daub, although work started on the stone-built house very shortly after their departure. The farm developed and prospered under Sir Richard's proprietorship.[29]

Although 'The Old Farm at Strawberry Hill' is now partly engulfed by modern housing, the site remains extremely evocative (Fig. 4). The farm is reached by a lane through a tangle of poplar trees, their bright yellow leaves drifting across the path of the approaching visitor, should he have a good fortune to time his visit for autumn, as he passes the crumbling stump of what is purported to be the remains of an elm-tree that was planted by Sir Richard. Lawns surround the cottage, and not far distant grow several very old pear trees. Inside, the building has been tastefully furnished with nineteenth century furniture by the National Trust of Western Australia who now own the property. The atmosphere is unequivocably English, and the cottage and garden stand in poignant contrast to the rounded granite boulders and eucalypts that form their backdrop on the northern side. One feels that the essential aura of the place has not changed so very greatly since Darwin and FitzRoy called on the Government Resident in 1836.

There was another interesting event that may have taken place on 7

March, the attendance by Darwin and FitzRoy, and probably many others of the ship's company of an Aboriginal corroboree. The time can be established, within fairly close limits, for Darwin records in his *Journal*:

> During the first two days after our arrival, there happened to be a large tribe called the White Cockatoo men, who came from a distance paying the town a visit. Both these men & the King George's Sound Men were asked to hold a 'Corrobery' or dancing party near one of the Resident's houses.

Whether 'the first two days' includes the 6 March, the actual day of the *Beagle*'s arrival, is not entirely clear, but as it does not seem that many of the crew went ashore that evening, perhaps not. Nor is it certain whether the phrase means two *complete* days — did the visiting Cockatoo people depart on the 8th, or early on the 9th? The 7th is the date suggested as the date for the corroboree, for Darwin seems to have undertaken extensive field-work and note-writing on Tuesday 8th — this is discussed below.

Charles merely states that the Aborigines 'were tempted with the offer of some boiled rice or sugar', but a comparison with Captain FitzRoy's account is interesting. He records that the corroboree was proposed because 'the residents wished to conciliate the "Cocotu" tribe'.[30] Also, even in his own *Journal* Charles appears reticent about his own generosity, for FitzRoy records that 'Mr Darwin secured the compliance of all the savages by providing an immense mess of boiled rice, with sugar for their entertainment.' He noted that 'About two hours after dark the affair began'; this may not contradict with Charles' observation that 'As soon as it grew dark they lighted small fires and commenced their toilet; this consisted of painting themselves . . .' particularly as the next sentence commences 'As soon as all was ready . . .'. As, at the end of the first week of March in southwestern Australia, sunset is at about 6.30 p.m. local time, we may assert with some confidence that Charles Darwin attended an Aboriginal corroboree at King George's Sound, commencing at about 8.30 p.m. on Monday 7 March 1836, preparations for the festivities having started about two hours earlier. The occasion, like all those in which he came into contact with 'primitive' human communities during the course of the voyage, has quite an effect upon him. His *Journal* account is worth quoting in its entirety:

> . . . their toilet . . . consisted of painting themselves in spots and lines with a white colour. As soon as all was ready, large fires were kept blazing, round which the women and children were collected as spectators. The Cockatoo and King George's men formed two distinct parties and danced generally in answer to each other. The dancing consisted in the whole set running either sideways or in Indian file into an open space and stamping the ground as they marched all together with great force. Their heavy footsteps were accompanied by a kind of

a grunt & by beating their clubs and weapons, & various other gesticulations, such as extending their arms and wriggling their bodies. It was a most rude and barbarous scene, & to our ideas without any sort of meaning; but we observed that the women and children watched the whole proceeding with the greatest pleasure. Perhaps these dances originally represented some scenes such as wars & victories; there was one called the Emu dance in which each man extended his arms in a bent manner, so as to imitate the movement of the neck of one of those birds. In another dance, one man took off all the motions of a kangaroo grazing in the woods, whilst a second crawled up & pretended to spear him. When both tribes mingled in one dance, the ground trembled with the heaviness of their steps & the air resounded with their wild crys. Everyone appeared in high spirits; & the group of nearly naked figures viewed by the light of the blazing fires, all moving in hideous harmony, formed a perfect representation of a festival amongst the lowest barbarians. [I imagine from what I have read that similar scenes may be seen amongst the same *coloured* people who inhabit the Southern extremity of Africa. *deleted*]. In T. del Fuego we have beheld many curious scenes of savage life, but I think never one where the natives were in such high spirits & so perfectly at their ease. After the dancing was over, the whole party formed a great circle on the ground & the boiled rice and sugar was distributed to the delight of all.

(Compare Darwin's descriptions of the King George's Sound Aborigines with the illustrations in Figs 5 and 6.)

Captain FitzRoy was also extremely interested in the Aboriginals and their customs and appearance. He devotes a good deal of space in his *Narrative* to a description of them, although he seems to have enjoyed the corroboree rather less than his young scientist colleague:

About two hours after dark the affair began. Nearly all the settlers, and their visitors, had assembled on a level place outside the village, while the native men belonging to both tribes were painting, or rather daubing and spotting their soot-coloured bodies with a white pigment, as they clustered round the blazing fires. When all was ready — the fires burning brightly — the gloom at a little distance intense, and the spectators collected together — a heavy tramp shook the ground, and a hundred prancing demon-like figures emerged from the darkness, brandishing their weapons, stamping together in exact accordance, and making hoarse guttural sounds at each exertion. It was a fiendish sight, almost too disagreeable to be interesting. What pains the savage man takes — in all parts of the world where he is found — to degrade his nature; that beautiful combination which is capable of so much intelligence and noble exertion when civilized and educated. While watching the vagaries of these performers, I could not but think of our imprudence in putting ourselves so completely in their

Figure 5—King George's Sound Aborigines at about the time of the *Beagle*'s visit: note the blackboys, and the outline of Bald Head in the background. From a print in Durmont D'Urville's *Voyage Pittoresque autour du Monde*, Paris, 1835.

Figure 6—King George's Sound and the Vancouver Peninsula in the 1830s. From a print in Durmont D'Urville's *Voyage Pittoresque autour du Monde*, Paris, 1835.

power: about thirty unarmed men being intermixed with a hundred armed natives. The dancers were all men; a short kangaroo-skin coat was thrown about their hips, and white feathers were stuck round their heads: many were not painted, but those who were had similar figures on their breasts; some a cross, others something like a heart. Many had spears, and all had the 'throwing-stick'; and a kind of hatchet, in a girdle round the waist. (This hatchet is made of two pieces of stone, joined together by a lump of gum, almost as hard as the stone; it is used for notching trees, that the men may climb after opposums.) Much of the dancing was monotonous enough, after the first appearance, reminding me of persons working in a treadmill: but their imitation of snakes and kangaroos, in a kind of hunting dance, was exceedingly good and interesting. The whole exhibition lasted more than an hour, during most of which time upwards of a hundred savages were exerting themselves in jumping and stamping as if their lives depended on their energetic movements. There was a boy who appeared to be idiotic, or afflicted with a kind of fit; but the man who was holding him seemed to be quite unconcerned . . . After the Corobbery the natives collected round the house where the feast was preparing; and it will not be easy to forget the screams of delight that burst from old and young as they looked in at the door and saw the tub in which their rice was smoking. Before the food was distributed they were told to sit down, which they immediately did, in a circle round the house. They separated, of their own accord, into families, each little party lighting a small fire before them. Their behaviour, and patience, were very remarkable and pleasing. One family had a native dog, which in size, colour, and shape was like a fox, excepting that the nose was not quite so sharp, nor the tail so bushy. (FitzRoy's Narrative, pp. 626-7)

The perceptive reader will have noticed significant differences between the two accounts. Certain details recorded by FitzRoy, and not in Darwin's account, enable us to gain a more complete and accurate idea of the corroboree. And the naval officer's comments on the Aboriginals would seem to be slightly more disparaging than those of his perhaps rather more progressive, scientific companion. The Captain's account includes rather more 'weighted' words: demon-like, fiendish, disagreeable, monotonous, savage, treadmill, idiotic. Darwin's attitude to the Aborigines will be briefly referred to again later.

At 9.00 a.m. on Tuesday 8 March it was a little warmer and less breezy than on the morning of the previous day. Captain FitzRoy's meteorological log records a moderate (Force 4) breeze from the south-east, blue skies with a few clouds, and an air temperature of 66 °F. Charles seems to have spent the day on a fairly thorough geological investigation of the area. His first draft of his account of the geology of the King George's Sound region is headed 'Tuesday'. It is written in a highly abbreviated form, and thus really constitutes a set of preliminary notes;[31] it is shown in Figure 7.

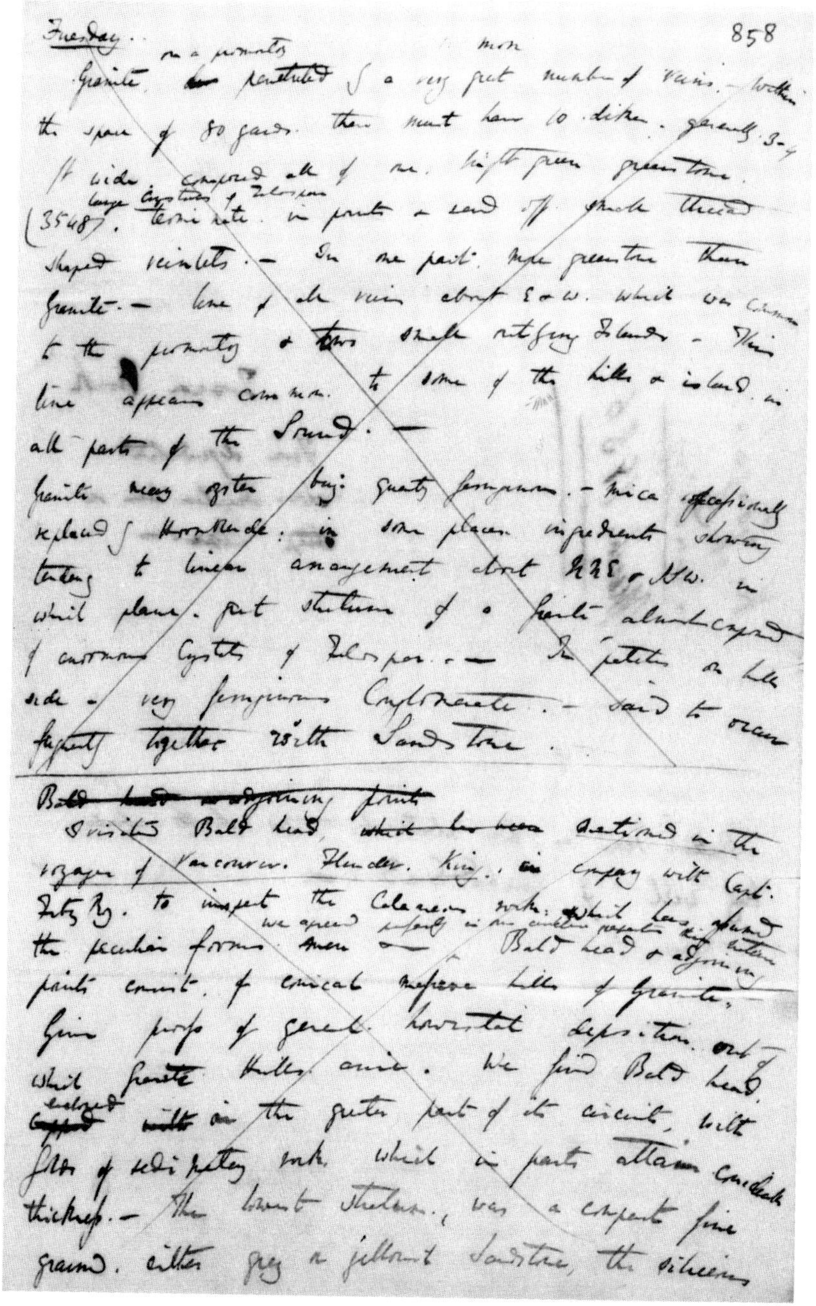

Figure 7—Darwin's preliminary notes on the Geology of the King George's Sound area. (Photograph: Cambridge University Library)

The first few lines of these annotations illustrate their general character and indicate the localities visited on the day in question:

> Tuesday
> Granite on a promontory penetrated by a very great number of veins — within the space of 100 yards there must have [been] 10 dikes, generally 3 or 4 ft wide, composed of bright green greenstone (3548). Large crystals of Feldspar terminate in points and send off small [?illegible] shaped veinlets — In one part more greenstone than granite. — Line of all veins about E & W which was common to the promontory & two outlying islands — This line appears common to some of the hills & islands in all parts of the Sound. — Granite near Oyster bay: quartz ferruginous — exceptionally replaced by Hornblende . . .

The promontory to which Charles refers is without doubt that now known as Vancouver Peninsula. This is a series of linked tombolos — islands joined to the mainland by low sandy ridges. These islands are of variable granitic rocks — in places white with large crystals of quartz and feldspar, but elsewhere richer in dark mafic minerals. The long axes of the islands run east west, and the granite is richly penetrated by veins. An outcrop of dolerite on Mistaken Island (which is mentioned by name in a later version of these notes, see p. 42) and also on the nearby peninsula perhaps explains Charles' mention of greenstone: it is in places well-rotted. If the *Beagle* were anchored a few hundred metres off the main settlement, the nearest point on the peninsula would have been less than about 3 km (approximately 1.8 miles) by ship's boat. (Fig. 8 shows some of the place names of the King George's Sound area.)

These notes on the 'promontory' are separated from the succeeding set of observations, those on Bald Head and its petrified trees, by a firm line across the page: possibly the former represent a morning excursion, the latter an afternoon trip. Darwin goes out of his way to say that Captain FitzRoy accompanied him on his investigation,[32] possibly because this was unusual on geological excursions.

> I visited Bald Head (which had been [deleted] mentioned in the Voyages of Vancouver, Flinders, King) in company of Captain FitzRoy to inspect the calcareous rock which has assumed peculiar forms. We agreed largely in our interpretation of this Question.

In the *Geological Diary*[33] (the more formal writing up of these preliminary notes, Figures 9 and 10) Charles is even more deferential to the view of his Captain.[34]

> I will particularly describe Bald Head — This spot has been known from the visits of the distinguished navigators, Vancouver, D'Entre-

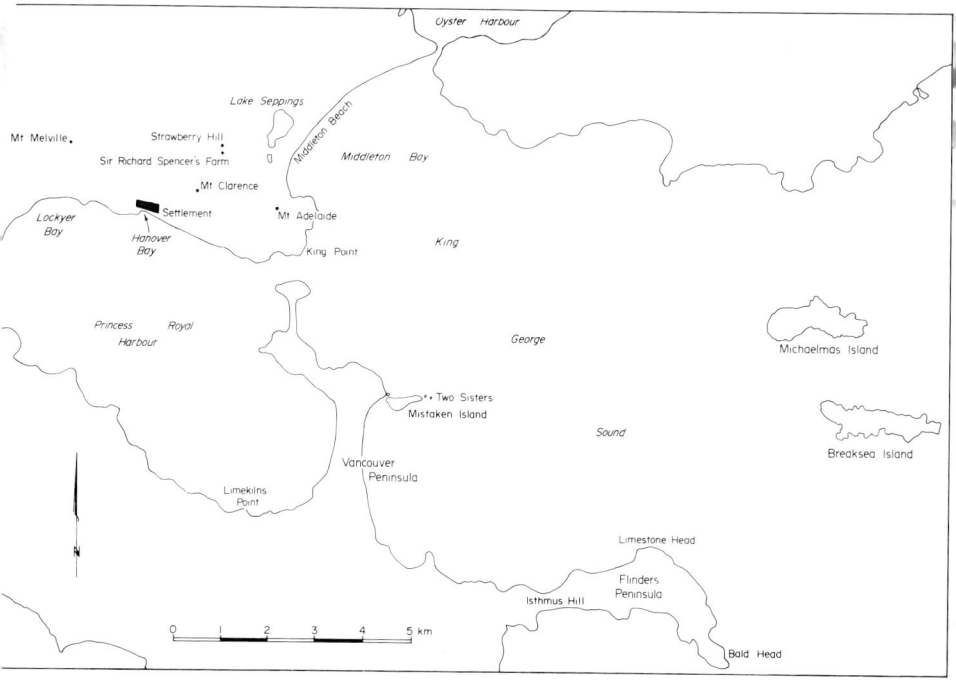

Figure 8—Some place names of the King George's Sound area.

casteaux, Freycinet, Flinders,[35] who have all mentioned with various opinions the singularly formed calcareous bodies lying on the ground. I went in the company of Capt. FitzRoy & as we perfectly coincided in opinion the following may be considered our joint observation on this disputed subject . . .

A little later he is careful to record that 'Capt. FitzRoy discovered a species of *Helix* and the case of an *Oniscus*'. A full account of the Bald Head site, and of its possible significance to Darwin will be given below (p. 46).

The carefully maintained meteorological log of the *Beagle* (Captain FitzRoy later became director of the antecedent of the Meteorological Office) records that at 9.00 a.m. on 9 March it was squally and the barometer had fallen slightly, although it was, at 68 °F, a little warmer than on the previous day. Charles Darwin carried forward his geological investigations, taking his written up geological notes of the previous day with him and annotating them, on the reverse, with further observations in pencil:

> 9th
> In front of ship, rocks slightly like gneiss, cleavage NNE, most obscure—a dozen dikes, parallel . . . found with [in] space of 100 yards, direction N by E . . .
> Further on, a mile, Gneiss, with very irregular cleavage, no fixed

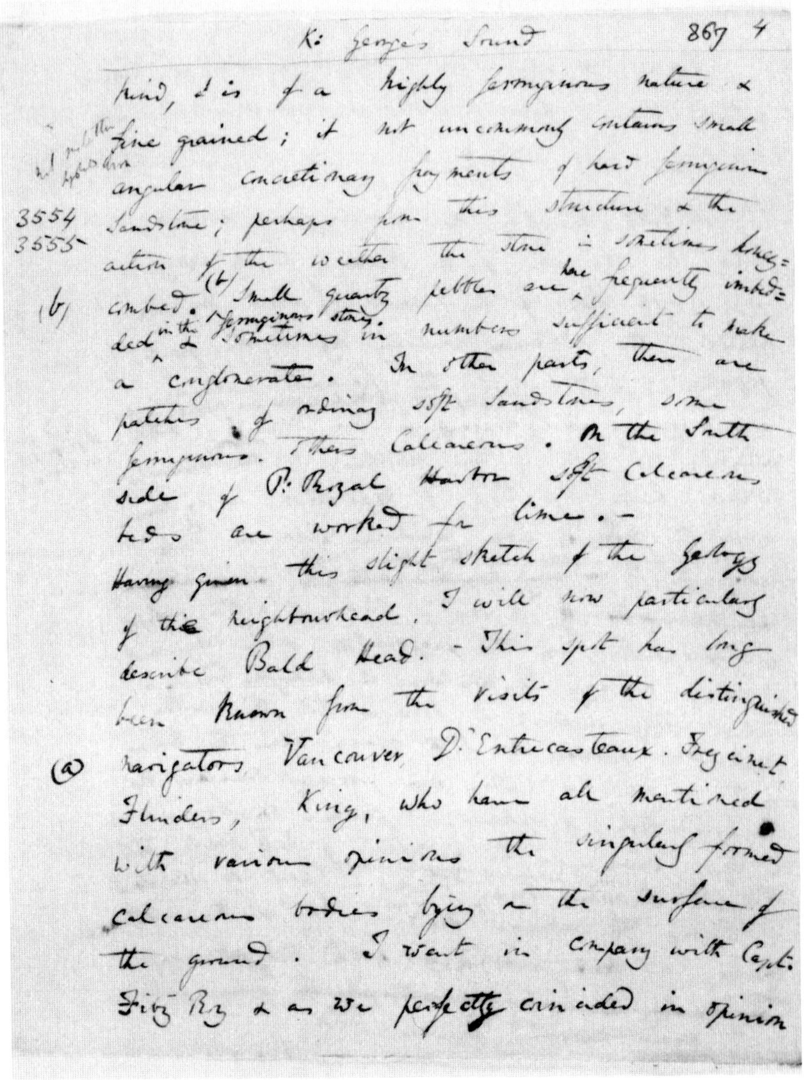

Figures 9 and 10—Pages from Charles Darwin's *Geological Diary* describe his visit, in the company of Captain FitzRoy, to Bald Head. (Photographs: Cambridge University Library)

K: George's Sound   868 (5

the following. may be considered our joint
observations on this disputed subject. —
As it appears to me, that there is sufficient
evidence to prove the origin of the strata,
in which the Calcareous bodies are imbedded
without at first in any way noticing their
presence, I shall proceed on this plan;
afterwards any arguments adduced from the
nature of the bodies themselves will chiefly
come in as support of such views. —

(a) Bald Head is a narrow steep sided ridge
about 600 ft high. — The fundamental rock is
Granite in its usual form of smooth stones.
These are encased to a considerable
thickness by layers of Calcareous matter either pure
or mixed with Sandstone. Strata accumulated
over narrow ridges & points must necessarily be
extremely irregular in form & thickness; I was
however surprised to find some inclined, with
an even surface at an angle of exactly
30 degrees. In many parts scarcely any stratification
could be perceived, in others seams (oblique to true strata)

direction ... I am doubtful whether this one does not belong to the granite formation ... Again soon saw some more dykes & some very gneiss-like granite.

These notes, suggesting a gradation between granite and gneiss, with the massive rocks traversed by numerous later intrusions, hint at considerable geological complexity.[36] They might refer to one of a number of localities in the King George's Sound area but in his full write-up of the region's geology Darwin states:

> .. Near the Settlement in Princess Royal Harbor, there is [a] ... system of 6 or 8 dikes; these are about a foot wide ... They occur within a hundred yards & run about N by E – S by W ...[37]

This must refer to the same site, and thus we can say with some certainty that the notes labelled '9th' were written while Darwin was walking along the northern shore of Princess Royal Harbour – Lockyer Bay, Hanover Bay, King Point. Unfortunately it is not easy to view many of the exposures today as the shore has been much altered and built-over since 1836. Where Charles Darwin once scrambled over the rocks with his geological hammer in hand, land has been reclaimed and grain storage bins, factories, warehouses, quays and railway sidings have been constructed.

On March 10 weather observations were not taken until noon, later than on the previous days. This no doubt explains why the air temperature was higher (70 °F). The barometer had fallen to 29.83 in., and although it was fine, it was squally and a Force 6 'strong breeze' was blowing from the west-nor'-west. By 6.00 p.m. this had grown to a 'moderate gale', Force 7. The very detailed statistical appendices to Captain FitzRoy's *Narrative* show that magnetic observations were made on March 10, again by Lt. Sullivan. FitzRoy noted:

> There is an extraordinary degree of local magnetic attraction about this place. We could not ascertain the amount of variation with any degree of accuracy until our compasses were placed upon a sandy beach of considerable extent,[38] near the sea. Wherever there was stone (a kind of granite) near the instruments, they were so much affected as to vary many degrees from the truth, and quite irregularly. (*Narrative*, p. 625)

Probably this is the reason that the observations of magnetic dip, variation and intensity made two days earlier were repeated. Surprisingly Darwin does not mention these magnetic anomalies in any of his writings. Probably he was not present when the observations were made, and in any case he does not seem to have had much interest in navigation: he would perhaps have seen magnetic measurement as a part of the seaman's craft,

Figure 11—Lake Seppings. (Photograph: Patrick Armstrong)

and not have considered the study of geomagnetism as the branch of the earth sciences that it much later became.

We cannot be sure exactly what itinerary was followed by Charles on March 10, or indeed on any of his last few days in Western Australia. He notes in the *Voyage*: 'One day I went out with a party in hopes of seeing a kangaroo hunt and walked over a good many miles of country'. He was disappointed, however, and although he mentions the vegetation he encountered (see p. 35) he found the landscape 'uninviting'.

Sometime during his stay he must have spent a certain amount of time collecting the fish and shells that represented the main zoological specimens gathered at King George's Sound, (see p. 8). Shells, including some of the same species collected by Darwin, may today be found in abundance on Middleton Beach, so it is possible that his specimens came from there. Most are annotated in his list (CULM/DAR 29.3, item 3/8) only as 'King George's Sound'. However, one is described as a 'Physa', freshwater lake, King George's Sound'. The only possible locality is Lake Seppings (Fig. 11), immediately inland from Middleton Beach.

The final few days—11, 12 and 13 March—must have been rather frustrating for the *Beagle*'s crew. Darwin's *Journal* records: 'Our departure was delayed by strong winds and cloudy weather'. The published version refers to 'several tedious delays'. In fact, on 11 March there was almost no wind,

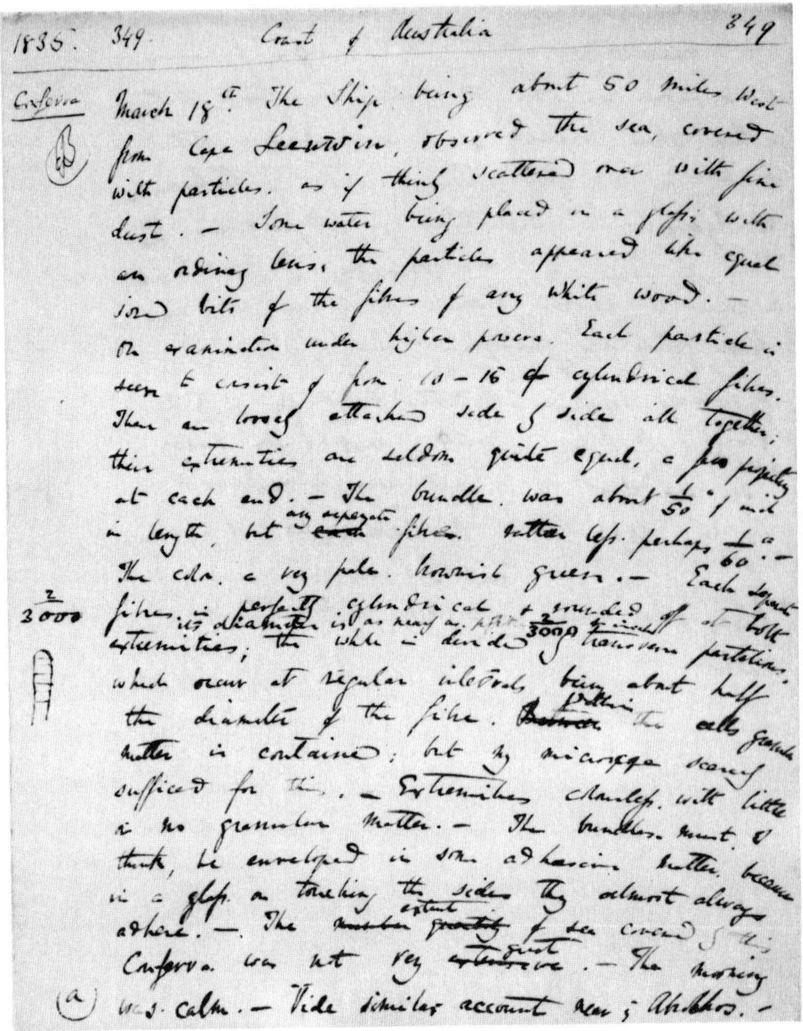

Figure 12—Charles Darwin's descriptions of phytoplankton off Cape Leeuwin, Western Australia. (Photograph: Cambridge University Library)

the weather being described as gloomy and threatening. By 9.00 a.m. on the following day a Force 5 west-nor'-west wind was blowing, and it was cloudy, gloomy and squally, with passing showers. On 13 March a Force 6 sou'-wester was blowing, and the weather remained rather poor. A study of Captain FitzRoy's barometer reading for the period 10–13 March suggests that a depression was passing slowly over the south-west of Australia: probably little useful scientific work was done during these last few days.

On 14 March, however, the glass was rising (the barometer reading was 30.32 in.), and the wind had moderated to Force 4, veered to the south, losing its westerly component: the *Beagle* 'stood out of King George's Sound, on ... course to Keeling Island'. Although gales and foul weather were experienced late in the passage (27 March onwards) the first part of the voyage seems to have been uneventful. However, the weather log records, enigmatically, that at 6.00 a.m. on 16 March, the vessel 'passed through a remarkable tide ripple or meeting of waters'. The *Beagle* was then about 100 miles (c. 150 km) south of Cape Leeuwin. Progress continued to be rather slow, the brig being propelled for the most part by Force 2 light breezes, and by 18 March, the *Beagle* was still only about 50 miles (c. 75 km) west of Cape Leeuwin. Here Darwin 'observed the sea covered with particles, as if thinly covered with fine dust'.[39]

These particles turned out to be confervae — minute plant organisms, Darwin's full account of which is given in the section immediately following. Suffice it to say here that the organism mentioned is almost certainly the blue-green alga *Trichodesmium*, which occurs quite frequently in cool tropical and warm temperate Indian Ocean waters. Strands a few metres wide but several kilometres in length have been noted in the waters off south-western Australia.

From this point Captain FitzRoy took a course almost due north-west to the Cocos Islands, and Charles Darwin lost sight of Western Australia for ever.

Chapter 3

DARWIN'S PERCEPTION OF THE WEST AUSTRALIAN ENVIRONMENT

IT IS SOMETIMES SAID that Charles was 'tired' in the last few months of the *Beagle*'s voyage. Although he frequently mentions his dislike of ships, and certainly missed his family — he noted in one of his letters home that he was planning the precise coaches he would catch to reach Shrewsbury in the shortest time possible after the ship berthed — there is little evidence that his powers of observation and deduction were in any way lower while he was in Western Australia than earlier in his travels. If one inspects the series of special red, paper-covered note-books[40] in which he kept his notes on geological specimens he collected, the sequence follows logically without interruption: there are details of fossils and rocks from South America, the Galapagos, New Zealand, New South Wales, Hobart Town, King George's Sound, Keeling, Mauritius, the Cape of Good Hope, and so on. The level of detail in the later entries is neither higher nor lower, and the succinct, clear descriptions are in the same form throughout. His account of the Bald Head site (discussed on p. 46) is particularly detailed and careful, and there would appear to be little criticism that could be made of the description of the confervae noticed just off the West Australian coast (see p. 29 and Fig. 12).

> Some water being placed in a glass, with an ordinary lens, the particles appeared like equal sized bits of fibres of any white wood — on examination under higher power, each particle is seen to consist of from 10-15 cylindrical fibres. These are loosely attached side by side all together; their extremities are seldom quite equal, a few projecting at each end. — The bundle was about 1/50th of inch in length, but any separate fibres rather less, perhaps 6/60th. — The colour, a very pale brownish green. Each separate fibre is perfectly cylindrical and rounded off at both extremities; its diameter is near 2/3000 an inch; the whole is divided by transverse partitions, which occur at regular intervals being about half the diameter of the fibre. Within the cells granular matter is contained; but any microscope is scarcely sufficient for this.
>
> Extremities colourless, with little or no granular matter — The bundles must, I think, be enveloped in some adhesive matter, because in a glass, on touching the sides they almost adhere. The extent of the sea

covered by this confervae was not very great — The morning was calm ...[41]

The level of detail, the powers of observation, appropriate scientific caution, careful statement of measurements and the conditions under which observations were made make this almost a model of scientific description.

In many ways Darwin was far ahead of his time, for he attached great importance in his notes to the *behaviour* of organisms, and their *relationships* with other organisms in their environment, almost a century before the sciences of ethology and ecology were developed.[42] The extract below is taken from his description of a giant crab found in the Keeling Islands,[43] and perhaps provides a better example of this type of writing than is to be found in his notes on the West Australian mainland. It is from the *Zoological Diary*[44] (see also Fig. 13).

> These monstrous crabs inhabit in numbers the low strips of dry coral land; they live entirely on the fruit of the cocoa nut tree. Mr Leisk informs me he has often seen them tearing, fibre by fibre, with their strong forceps, the husks of the nut. This process they always perform at the extremity, where their three eyes are situated. By constant hammering the shell in that soft part is broken & then by the aid of their narrow posterior pincers the food is extracted. I think this is as curious a piece of adaptation and instinct as I ever heard of. The crabs are diurnal in their habits; they live in burrows which frequently lie at the foot of the trees. Within the cavity they collect a pile, sometimes as much as a large bag full of the picked fibre and husks & on this they rest. At night they are said to travel to the sea: there also the young are hatched & during the early part of their life they remain & probably feed on the beach. Their flesh is very good food: in the tail of a large one is a lump of fat which when melted down gives a bottle full of oil. They are exceedingly strong. — The back is coloured dull brick red: the under side of the body & legs is blue, but the upper side of the legs clouded with dull red. In the 'Voyage par un Officier du Roi' to the Isle of France[45] there is an account of a crab which lives on Cocoa Nuts in a small island North of Madagascar: probably it is the same animal, but the account is very imperfect.
>
> Mr Liesk informs me that the crabs with swimming plates to posterior claw employ this tool in excavating burrows in the fine sand and mud & that he has repeatedly watched the process.

In this account of one of his specimens (number 1428), notes on morphology and habitat are thus carefully linked with descriptions of behaviour. Also a full description of the organism itself is complemented by a comparison with records from elsewhere (his own observations being carefully distinguished from those of others). This comparison of the organisms of

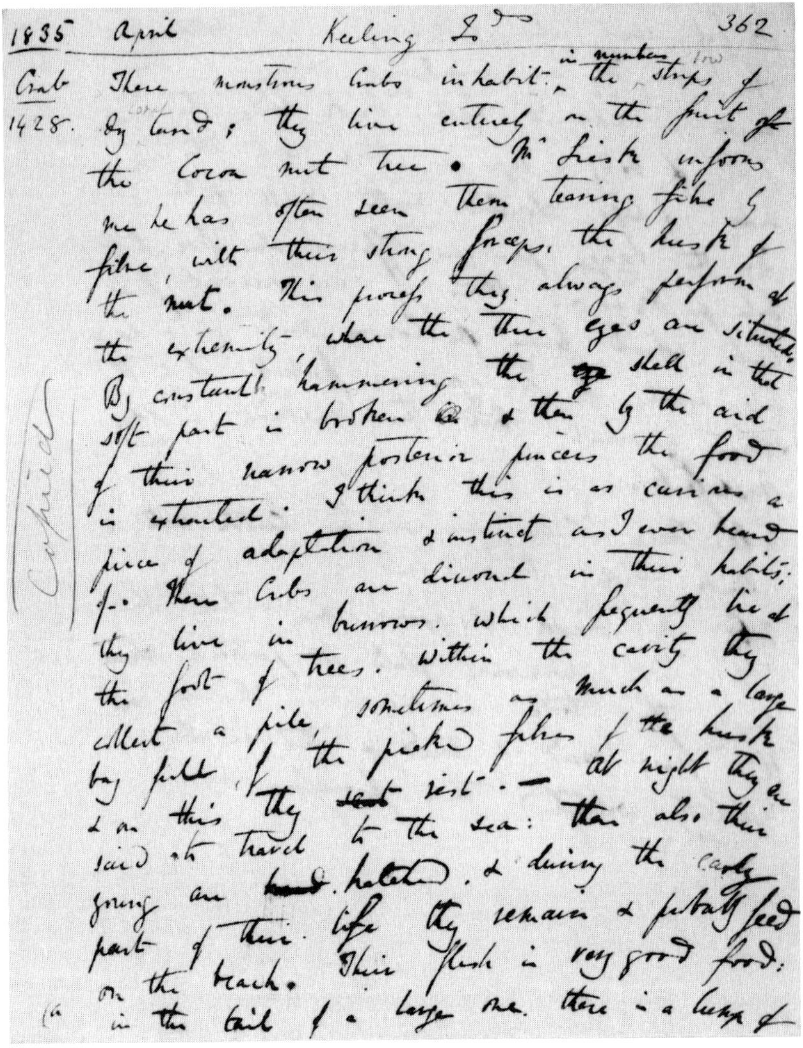

Figure 13—Darwin's description of crabs in the Cocos (Keeling) Islands. (Photograph: Cambridge University Library)

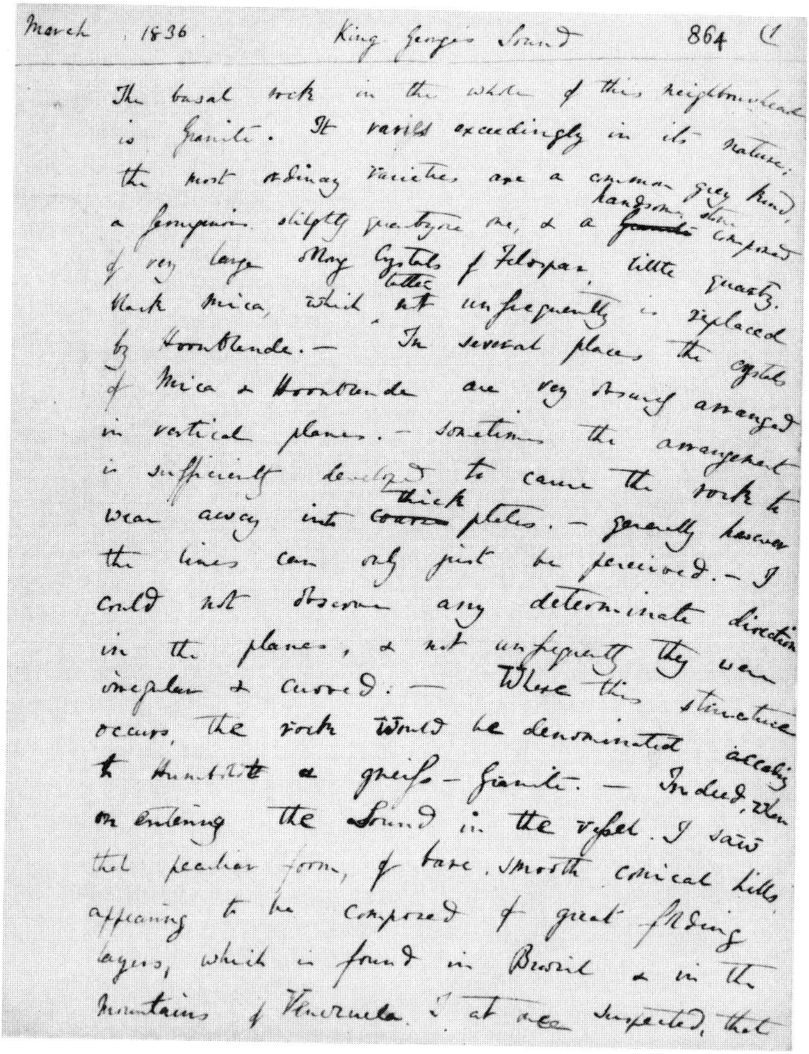

March 1836.   King George's Sound   864

The basal rock in the whole of this neighbourhead is Granite. It varies exceedingly in its nature; the most ordinary varieties are a common grey kind, a ferruginous slightly quartzose one, & a handsome kind composed of very large shiny Crystals of Felspar, little quartz, black mica, which, not unfrequently is replaced by Hornblende. — In several places the crystals of Mica & Hornblende are very strongly arranged in vertical planes. — Sometimes the arrangement is sufficiently developed to cause the rock to wear away into thick plates. — generally however the lines can only just be perceived. — I could not discover any determinate direction in the planes, & not unfrequently they were irregular & curved. — Where this structure occurs, the rock would be denominated locally Hornblende & gneiss-Granite. — Indeed, when on entering the Sound in the vessel I saw that peculiar form, of bare, smooth conical hills, appearing to be composed of great folding layers, which is found in Brazil & in the Mountains of Venezuela; at once suspected, that

Figure 14—Part of Darwin's description of King George's Sound from his *Geological Diary*. (Photograph: Cambridge University Library)

Figure 15—Close up of granite from the King George's Sound area: 'a handsome stone composed of very large crystals of feldspar, little quartz, black mica, which latter infrequently replaced by hornblende'. (Photograph: Patrick Armstrong)

one locality with those of another marks much of the *Beagle* and post-*Beagle* writings, and his interest in the distribution of plants and animals was a fundamental component in the development of the species theory.[46]

A similar precision characterises his geological observations. For example here are the opening lines of his report on King George's Sound from his *Geological Diary*, see Figures 14 and 15:

> **March 1836   King George's Sound**
>
> The basal rock in the whole of this neighbourhood is granite. It varies exceedingly in its nature; the most ordinary varieties are a common grey kind, a ferruginous, slightly quartzose one, and a handsome stone composed of very large oblong crystals of feldspar, little quartz, black mica, which latter infrequently is replaced by Hornblende. — In several places the crystals of Mica and Hornblende are very obscurely arranged in vertical planes. — Sometimes the arrangement is sufficiently developed to cause the rock to wear away into thick plates — generally, however the lines can only just be perceived. I could not observe any determinate direction in the planes, & not infrequently they were irregular and curved. Where this structure occurs, the rock would be denominated according to Humboldt[47] a gneiss-granite. Indeed on entering the sound in the Vessel, I saw that peculiar form of bare smooth conical hills appearing to be composed of great folding layers,[48] which is found in Brazile & in the Mountains of Venezuela, I at once suspected that the observation of Humboldt of the frequency of this form in the hills of gneiss-granite, would be verified in this part of Australia.[49]

Yet despite his eye for detail, revealed in some of the above extracts, Darwin also had the ability to assess and convey with remarkable succinctness, the totality of a landscape or environment. Here is his account of the landscape around King George's Sound:

> The country viewed from an eminence, appears a woody plain, with here & there rounded and partly bare hills of granite . . . Everywhere we found the soil sandy & very poor; either supported a coarse vegetation of low brushwood & wiry grass, or a forest of stunted trees. The scenery resembled the elevated sandstone platform of the Blue Mountains[50]. The Casuarina (a tree which somewhat resembles a Scotch fir) is, however, in rather greater proportion as the eucalyptus is rather less. In the open parts there are great numbers of grass-trees which in appearance have some affinity with the palm, but instead of a crown of noble leaves, it can boast merely a tuft of coarse grass. The general bright green colour of the brushwood & other plants viewed from a distance seems to bespeak fertility; a single walk will, however, dispel any such illusion . . . all the broad flat bottomed valleys which are covered with rush-like grasses and brushwood, are in winter so

swampy as scarcely to be passable ... The settlement consists [of] from 30-40 small white washed cottages, which are scattered on the side of a bank & along a white sea beach. (*Journal*, p. 392)

(The account was slightly edited when reproduced for publication in the *Voyage*. Fig. 16 shows the scrubby vegetation and rounded granite hilltops of the King George's Sound landscape, and Fig. 17 a photograph of the grass trees.)

In immediately characterising the environment as sandy and infertile, Darwin was acting with far more percipience than, for example, had Captain Stirling, less than a decade earlier, in his evaluation of the Swan River region. Some of the results of that inaccurate assessment were tragic.

Throughout his travels, Darwin was intensely interested in the 'primitive' human communities with whom he came into contact. He goes into considerable detail, in his *Journal* on the inhabitants of Tierra del Fuego, the Pacific Islands and New South Wales. The Aborigines of King George's Sound were no exception. A detailed account of a corroboree he attended has already been given (p. 17). Typically, he compared West Australian Aborigines with people he had encountered elsewhere. In comparing King George's Sound with the eastern colonies he commented first on the more pleasant, moister climate, and then went on:

Figure 16—Rounded granite hilltops and scrub-covered valleys of the King George's Sound area. (Photograph: Patrick Armstrong)

Figure 17—Western Australian grass tree (*Xanthorrhoea preissii*).

> The second grand advantage is the good disposition of the aboriginal blacks; it is not easy to imagine a more truly good natured & good humoured expression than their faces show. Moreover they are quite willing to work & make themselves very useful; in this respect they are very different from the other Australian colonies. In their habits, manners, instruments and general appearance they resemble the natives of New South Wales. Like them they are very remarkable by the extreme slightness of their limbs, especially their legs; yet without as it would appear, muscles to move their legs, they will carry a burden for a longer time than most white men. Their faces are very ugly, the beard is curly & not at all deficient, the skin of the whole body is very hairy & their persons abominably filthy. Although true savages, it is impossible not to feel an inclination to like such quiet good-natured men. (*Journal*, p. 392)

Typical Darwin this — the comparative treatment, the eye for detail, the hint of scientific caution. Yet, scientist though he is, Charles is also a child of his time, and sees the Aboriginal people of Western Australia from the standpoint of an upper middle-class, European set of values. He refers to them as 'true Savages', he feels it 'abominable' that they should be so 'filthy', and he regards willingness to work as an important criterion on which to base an evaluation, yet he admires their strength and their quiet, easy-going, friendly nature. In this he was perhaps more progressive than the conservative Captain FitzRoy who could not conceal his unease at being present at a corroboree 'with a hundred armed natives', and who described the occasion as 'a fiendish sight — almost too disagreeable to be interesting' (see p. 18).

Darwin also tries to be reasonably objective in his evaluation of the white colonists and their activities:

> Certainly I formed a low opinion of the place; it must, however, be remembered that only from two to three years have elapsed since its effectual colonization[51] & for this great allowances must be made.

He noted the 'nice farm' of one landowner, but referred to the town having an 'uncomfortable appearance'. He seemed grudgingly to appreciate the colonists' lack of dependance upon the 'cheap labour of convicts' — an aspect of life in New South Wales that he deplored — yet he had doubts as to whether the fledgling colony would survive:

> The inhabitants live on salted meat & of course have no fresh meat or vegetables to sell; they do not even take the trouble to catch the fish with which the bay abounds: indeed I cannot make out what they intend doing. (*Journal*)

On the whole, however, for someone of his era (Queen Victoria had not even come to the throne by the time H.M.S. *Beagle* was moored safely back in the River Thames), Charles Darwin seems remarkably free from prejudice, willing to give credit where credit is due, to black or white, rich or poor. His enlightened views were probably in the minority amongst the officers of the *Beagle*.

He had, in fact, a rather ambivalent attitude to Australia as a whole. In his letter to his friend and teacher, Professor Henslow, from Sydney he wrote:

> You see we are now arrived in Australia: the new Continent really is a wonderful place. Ancient Rome might have boasted of such a colony; it deserves to rank high amongst the 100 wonders of the world, as showing the Giant force of the parent country. The system of communications is carried out on an admirable scale; the roads are excellent & on the Macadam principle; to form them vast masses of rock are cut away. The following facts I think, very forcibly show how rapid & extraordinary is the increase in wealth—a fraction (I believe 7/8) of an acre of land in Sydney fetched by Auction twelve thousand pounds; the increase of public revenue during the last year has been 68,000£.—It is well known, that there are men, who came out convicts who now possess a yearly income of 15,000£. Is not this all wonderful? But I do not think this country can ever rise to be a second North America. The sterile aspect of the land, at once proclaims that Agriculture will never succeed. Wool ... must ever be the cry from one end of the country to the other ... On the whole I do not like New South Wales; it is no doubt an admirable place to accumulate pounds and shillings; but Heaven forbid that ever I should live, where every man is sure to be somewhere between a petty rogue & bloodthirsty villain. (Letter 41, *Darwin and Henslow*, see footnote 2)

If anything his summary of King George's Sound was even less favourable, despite the absence of convicts:

> I do not remember, since leaving England, having passed a more dull, uninteresting time.
>
> He who thinks with me, will never wish to walk again in so uninviting a country. (*Voyage*)

His letter to his sister Caroline, from Port Louis, Mauritius, dated 29 April 1836, is just as definite:

> I wrote from Sydney and Hobart Town. After leaving the latter place, we proceeded to King George's Sound. I did not feel much affection for any part of Australia, and certainly nothing would be better adapted, than our last visit, to put the finishing stroke on such feelings. (CULM/DAR 223)

Library of
Davidson College

However, he certainly felt that Western Australia had prospects:

> I understand & believe it true, that thirty miles inland there is excellent land for all purposes: this is already granted into allotments & will soon be under cultivation. The settlement of King George's Sound will ultimately be the Sea port of this inland district. (*Journal*)

And on leaving Western Australia:

> Farewell Australia, you are a rising child and doubtless will reign a great princess in the South; but you are too great and ambitious for affection, yet not great enough for respect; I leave your shore without sorrow or regret. (*Voyage*)

Whatever one feels about Charles' lack of affection for Australia in general and Western Australia in particular, one cannot but admire the remarkable prescience of some of his remarks!

Although therefore, Charles Darwin's *Voyage of the Beagle* account of this small corner of Western Australia was brief, by comparing it with the observations of Captain FitzRoy, and supplementing it with details derived from Darwin's notes, it is possible to say quite a lot about the way in which he saw King George's Sound in March 1836. His powers of observation, his attention to detail, his ability to assess an environment perceptively and sum up its chief characteristics succinctly, and his intense interest in the plants, animals, soils, rocks and landscapes of the area were typical of the spirit of inquiry that characterised all of his work. His attitudes to the European and Aboriginal inhabitants were of course to some extent constrained by the mores of the era and also to some degree by his upbringing. Yet his concern for accuracy, careful scrutiny of information given by others, his sometimes brilliant comparative approach, his ability to see often obscure relationships, and his respect for 'all sorts and conditions of men', displayed in his annotations on Western Australia shine out against the background of a time often characterised by ignorance, prejudice, parochialism and dogmatism. He did not like Western Australia, yet some of his prognosis has proved remarkably accurate.

Chapter 4

GEOLOGICAL INVESTIGATIONS

ALTHOUGH CHARLES' ENTHUSIASM for the various branches of natural history fluctuated a little throughout his voyage, his interest in geology was maintained at a high level in most of the places at which the *Beagle* called. We have already seen that he collected few, if any, birds or reptiles in Western Australia, yet his notes on the geological sites that he visited while his ship lay at anchor in King George's Sound are copious. He collected rocks and fossil specimens, carefully recording each of them in one of the paper-covered notebooks that he kept for the purpose, with exemplary constancy throughout the journey, and even his letters to his family mention some of his enthusiasm for geology. A letter from his sister (dated 12 February 1836, his twenty-seventh birthday) is interesting:

> ... I am as much delighted as any of them [Charles' family] at your present success and future prospects of distinguishing yourself in Geology. I was reading the other day part of your early journal, just before you left Plymouth when you made yourself an outline of how you meant to pass your time, & amongst your studies I was surprised to find no mention of Geology, but this must have been an oversight, because just after your tour with Professor Sedgwick you must have been hot on the subject.

It goes on, in a typically concerned way:

> I hope you won't go exploring too boldly in New Holland as I think land dangers are more to be dreaded than sea ones.

Not for the last time Australia seems to have got a bad press! Many of Charles' geological observations were published in the three volumes of the *Geology of the Voyage*, on Coral Islands, Volcanic Islands and South America (footnote 19). His material on King George's Sound did not fit comfortably under any of these headings, but although he makes brief reference to his Australian fieldwork in all three volumes, he includes a short section at the end of the Volcanic Islands volume that he prefaces as follows:

> The *Beagle* on her homeward voyage, touched at New Zealand, Australia, Van Diemen's Land and the Cape of Good Hope. In order to

Figure 18—'The hills of granite are seen abruptly to rise out of a plain'. Steep-sided, rounded granite domes form a backdrop to the present-day town of Albany, Western Australia. (Photograph: Patrick Armstrong)

> confine the third part of these geological observations of South America, I will here briefly describe all that I observed at these places worthy of the attention of geologists. (*Volcanic Islands*, p. 130)

His description of King George's Sound occupies about six pages of this section. It commences with a description of the underlying granite — a shortened version of the notes quoted on page 35. He goes on:

> These plutonic rocks are in many places, intersected by trappean dikes: in one place I found ten parallel dikes, ranging in an E and W line; and not far off another set of eight dikes composed of a different variety of trap, ranging at right angles to the former ones.

Again, this represents a ruthless compression of his preliminary notes, mentioned on page 22, and of the fair copy in the *Geological Diary*:

> The granitic rocks are traversed by a multitude of veins of different varieties, some of which appear contemporaneous & others injected. There are also a great many dikes of Trappean stones at the Eastern Extremity of Mistaken Isle. There are, within the space of about a

hundred yards, about ten dikes, each from 3 to 4 ft thick and composed of the same kind of bright green stone, containing rather large Crystals of Feldspar. Some of the dikes terminate in wedge-shaped points and throw off thin veins. In one part they were in such close proximity, that the Greenstone in quantity exceeded the proportions of Granite. The dikes are nearly parallel & run about E & W; this is the direction of the point & of some of the outlying rocks & islands— This line is likewise common to several of the hills & Islands near the Sound.

Incorporating the material in rough notes, probably written on 9 March, the third day of fieldwork, and almost certainly with the appropriate specimens on the chart table in the cabin of the *Beagle* before him, he went on:

Near the settlement in Princess Royal Harbor, there is another system of six or eight dikes; these are a foot wide with a structure slightly prismatic, & composed of a black base, prophyritic with very numerous small crystals of glittering Feldspar & some Iron pyrites. They occur within a space of a hundred yards & run about N by E—S by W; a direction at right angles to the last system. Besides these I noticed

Figure 19—'The granitic rocks are traversed ... by dikes ... 3 to 4 ft thick'. A dyke intruded into granite on the south side of Princess Royal Harbour. Bald Head in the background. (Photograph: Patrick Armstrong)

Figure 20—Exposure of calcareous sandstone in the flanks of Bald Head, possibly that visited by Darwin and FitzRoy. (Photograph: Patrick Armstrong)

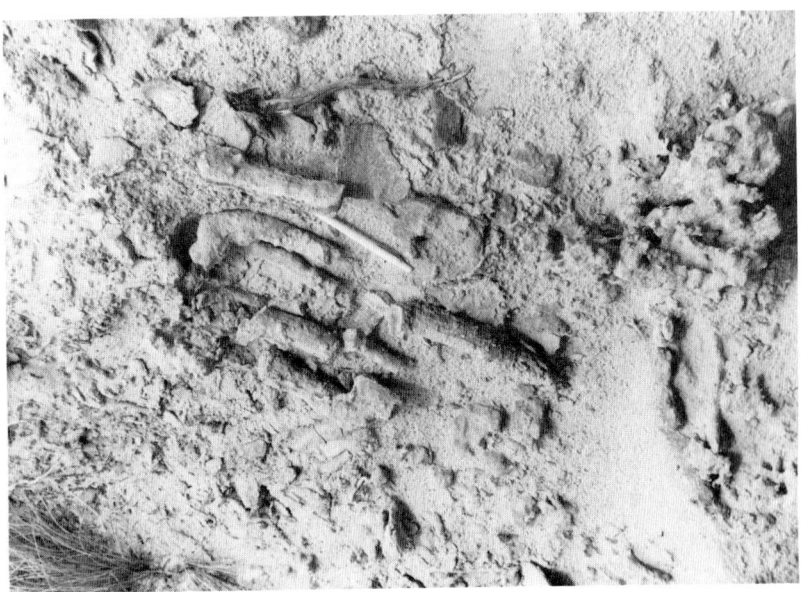

Figure 21—'Peculiar calcareous cylindrical projections, which originally were mistaken for coral ..., occur all over the promontory of Bald Head.' Today these would be described as *rhizoconcretions*. (Photograph: Patrick Armstrong)

Figure 22—At Bald Head today there are few rhizoconcretions 'remaining in the position of growth' although these can be seen elsewhere. Those above are in sand dunes near Eucla, Western Australia. The knife is 22 cm in length. (Photograph: Patrick Armstrong)

> several scattered dikes, also some masses of Greenstone (3552, 3553); which I am ignorant whether they belong to the age of the dikes or of the Granites. From their containing, however, very heavy grains of quartz, I should suppose the latter.

At this point in the *Geological Diary*, Darwin's flair for grasping and succinctly describing a whole picture again becomes apparent:

> Viewing the country from an eminence, the hills of Granite are seen abruptly to rise out of a plain. Although the country is strictly a plain, yet from the many small valleys of excavation it is far from level. The granitic formation is everywhere in the low country smoothed over by sedimentary deposits.

Darwin noted that the most abundant sedimentary rock overlying the granitic basement was a sandstone (3554, 3555) which was:

> ... of a highly ferruginous nature, and fine grained; it not uncommonly contains some angular concretionary fragments of hard ferruginous sandstone; perhaps from this structure and the action of the weather this stone is sometimes honeycombed.[52]

Darwin here later inserted a marginal note, comparing this deposit with rocks described by Dr Fritton, in the appendix to Captain P. P. King's *Australia*.[53] The Ship's Naturalist of the *Beagle* is very cautious about the origin of these ferruginous sandstones. Even in the published version[54] he simply states:

> The origin of these superficial beds, though sufficiently obscure, seem to be due to alluvial action on detritus abounding with iron.

A modern geomorphologist would attribute much of the sandy material to Quaternary, perhaps largely Holocene, beach and dune deposits, with some slight admixture of lagoonal and estuarine deposits.

The site in Western Australia, indeed perhaps in the whole of Australia, that most impressed Charles Darwin was that of Bald Head. He covered 14 pages of 'fair copy' notes[55] on this site (see Figs 9, 10, 20, 21 and 22), and what is given here is considerably edited:

> Bald Head is a narrow steep-sided ridge 600 ft high. The fundamental rock is granite in its usual form of smooth obtuse cones. These are encased to a considerable thickness by layers of calcareous matter, either pure or mixed with sandstone. Strata accumulated over narrow ridges ... must necessarily be irregular in form & thickness; I was however surprised to find some inclined at an angle of exactly 30 degrees. In many places scarcely any stratification could be perceived ... other seams (oblique to the true strata) were inclined towards the hill ... The lowest rock I could see, was a ... compact fine grained grey or cream coloured sandstone ... In one spot was a Calcareous sandstone. I believe ... sandstones and hard stalactiform limestone ... alternate.

Darwin went on to argue, both in his notes and in the published version, that the deposits were largely wind-blown, fragments of shells being incorporated in the sand. The hard 'stalactitic' layers of limestone, into which sandy or 'earthy' deposits sometimes blended, he supposed:

> must ... as certain vein-like masses have been formed by rain dissolving the calcareous matter and re-precipitating it ... These layers are sometimes brecciated and recemented, as if they had been broken by the slipping of the sand when soft. I did not find a single fragment of

sea-shell; but bleached shells of *Helix melo*, an existing land species, abound in the all of the strata; and I likewise found ... the case of an *Oniscus* [woodlouse].[56]

Charles devoted considerable space in his notes to the petrified trees associated with the Bald Head calcareous deposit. His account is the customary blend of careful detailed observation and shrewd deduction.

> I will now describe the peculiar calcareous cylindrical projections, which originally[57] were mistaken for coral still remaining in the position in which it grows. These bodies occur all over the promontary of Bald Head ... I will only attempt to describe their appearance by stating [that] on Capt. FitzRoy pointing out certain ones lying on the ground, I was unable, before touching them, to say whether they were the actual roots of bushes, or calcareous models imitating such forms. Their general diameter is from that of a finger to the waiste ... The most common position is vertical, however, many are inclined; the greater number of branch downwards like roots. — I saw on the side of a little cliff, one very tortuous one, which extended in a perpendicular direction upwards of 3 ft in the ground; others again were suddenly bent in a horizontal line, after the manner of a root when it meets an obstacle in its course. In one great bare spot, where decomposed sandstone had been removed by the wind, these branches ... projected upward to the height of a foot. They were so close together that it was impossible to avoid .. breaking at each step ... These cylindrical models are generally composed either of white friable calcareous rock or the stalactiform kind; this latter frequently forms only the axis ... Land shells are not infrequently found attached to the outer coating ... Calcareous matter has filled up the cavity left by a decayed root or branch. In true petrification, every particle of organic matter is separately replaced by one of stone; but in this case the whole ... has been removed before stony matter was washed in by the rains. It will be observed that this view strongly agrees with the idea of the strata being consolidated matter of sand dunes.[58]

Darwin was convinced that these processes had been at work over several centuries of land uplift; the land had formerly, as he put it, 'stood lower in relation to the sea'.

> As the land rose, during the periods of its elevation, sand dunes would accumulate lower and lower on the flanks of the hills; in them bushes would grow and land shells abound. By degrees, the sand becoming solidified, the shells would be imbedded and the bushes would perish; their decayed roots and branches would then become so many casts to be occupied by calcareous matter. Hence not only at the summit, but the sides of the hills for some way downwards, are encased with this formation.[59]

As to whether these processes were still in operation, Darwin seems ambivalent! He continues: 'I [do not] believe, but am far from feeling sure, that this process is [*deleted* not] going on at this present day. The 'do not' is a later insertion, the second 'not' is deleted in pencil! In his published description, although by means of elaborate footnoting he compares the deposits with sites he had visited elsewhere or seen described in the literature, he does not commit himself on this last point.

In many ways Darwin's opinions of the geology of the King George's Sound area would coincide remarkably closely with those of modern scientists. He seems to have appreciated the relationship that exists between granite and gneiss (see p. 26) — that they grade into one another, and also the nature of the intrusive dikes (p. 43). But it was his appreciation of the nature of the Bald Head sandstones and limestones, and the plant material preserved in them, that was particularly perceptive. His deduction that the sandy deposits with confused cross or current-bedding, some at as much as 30° to the horizontal were wind-blown was entirely accurate. The 'hard stalactiform limestone' that occurred in layers in the sandy deposit would today be described as calcrete. However, his suggestion that it was formed through 'rain dissolving the calcareous matter and reprecipitating it', while broadly correct, might today be regarded as something of a simplification. Calcrete formation in the Quaternary coastal sand dunes in southwestern Western Australia has recently been investigated by V. Semeniuk, and T. D. Meagher,[60] who describe it as 'a capillary-rise phenomenon associated with plants'. Calcrete is forming today as a sheet 10–50 cm in thickness just above the water table in the barrier sand dunes of the southwest of Australia. Semeniuk and Meagher state that it is forming in response to the evapo-transpiration regime (i.e. total water-loss by evaporation and transpiration, from both ground surface and plants). The annual rainfall is quite high (827 mm per annum at Albany) but concentrated into just a few months: water infiltrates into the sand rapidly. High summer temperatures (January mean maximum, 27 °C at Albany) and evaporation, together with wind stress near the sea provide a 'water vapour deficit' above the dunes. To this the scrub vegetation responds by drawing on the 'vadose' or 'free' water above the water table, and the 'phreatic' water below it, and as the water is drawn away, the calcium carbonate is precipitated.

Darwin's 'petrified trees' would today be described as 'rhizoconcretionary calcrete': this forms as plants use up all the water in the vadose or upper zone during the hot summer, and the calcrete is precipitated around the roots. 'Plant roots remain alive even if encased by a calcrete annulus (up to) 2 mm thick'.[61] Eventually, however, the root dies, and exactly as Darwin described, the hollow becomes infilled with precipitated calcareous material. In the past successive dune surfaces may have been overwhelmed by mobile sand, resulting in the burial of surfaces, and the entombment of 'fossil' calcrete layers. Alternatively wind may remove superficial material to expose a filigree of contorted, branching rhizoconcretions at the surface, brittle rods of calcium carbonate, easily breaking when touched or trodden upon: both have occurred at this site. Alas there are few places today on Bald Head (the Flinders Peninsula) where the 'petrified roots' are as closely packed as they were in Darwin's day — many have been knocked down or destroyed. But places do exist elsewhere in southwestern Australia (compare Fig. 22) where they are 'so close together with it [is] impossible to avoid . . . breaking [them] at each step'. However, there are a number of overhangs on the north side of the peninsula (near Limestone Head) where, 20-30 m above sea level, light grey rhizoconcretions are weathering out of the creamy-yellow sand. Many are horizontal, and the texture of the original roots can be seen. In places the sand has been worn away so that elaborately convoluted 'serpentine' roots, sometimes branching, may be found. The concretions vary from 0.5-10 cm in thickness (see Fig. 21).

In one locality, about 2 km west of Limestone Head, the rounded surface of much veined granite can be seen, just above sea level, overlain by the sandy limestone. The most easterly point of the peninsula — Bald Head itself — is a rounded grey granite dome. Darwin's appraisal of the structure of the headland would appear to be entirely accurate, although he was wrong in implying that there had been a recent fall in sea level. The modern view is that the level has remained approximately constant for several millennia, but that there has previously been a rise in sea level, as the ice masses melted at the end of the Pleistocene glacial period, some 20,000-10,000 years ago. This rise was the cause of the formation of Princess Royal Harbour and King George's Sound itself, and the isolation of islands such as Michaelmas, Breaksea and Mistaken Isles through the drowning of a system of pre-existing valleys.

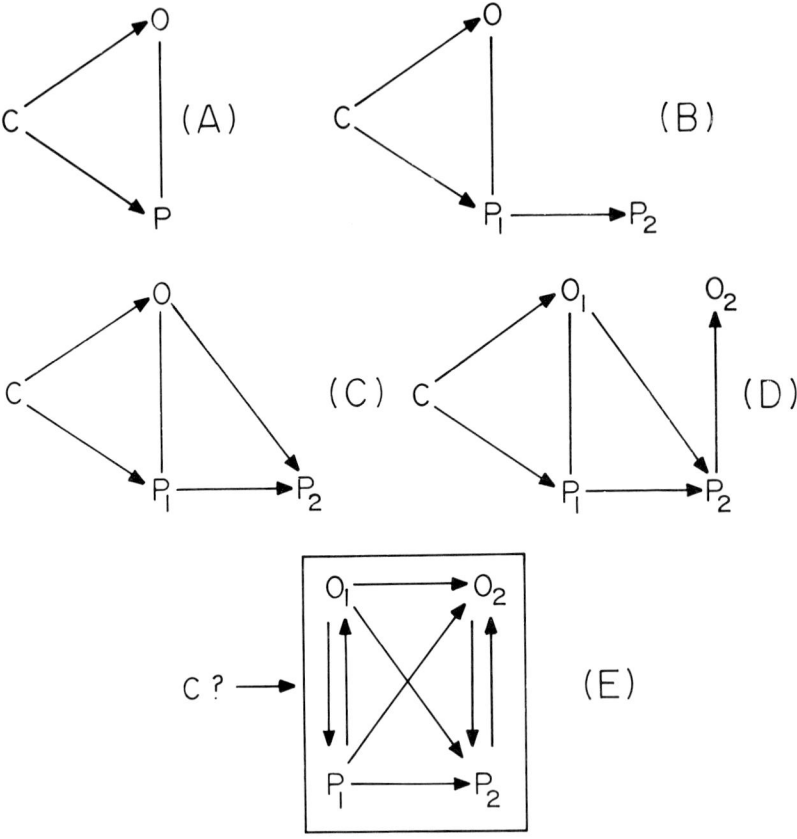

Figure 23—Darwin's changing view of the world. **A.** 1832 AND BEFORE. The Creator (C) made an organic world (O) and a physical world (P). O is perfectly adapted to P

B. 1832–1834 (DURING GEOLOGICAL EXPLORATIONS IN S. AMERICA). The physical world undergoes continuous change governed by natural laws summarised in Lyell's *Principles of Geology*

C. 1835 (THE PACIFIC). The activities of living organisms contribute to the evolution of the physical world, as exemplified by the action of coral organisms in building coral reefs

D. 1836–1837 (THE VOYAGE HOME AND AFTER). Changes in the physical world imply changes in the organic world if adaptation is to be maintained; the physical milieu induces appropriate biological adaptations

E. 1838 AND AFTER. The physical and organic worlds are continuously evolving and interacting with each other. The Creator, if he exists, may have set the natural systems in being, but does not interfere with its operation

(After Howard Gruber)

Chapter 5

THE EFFECT OF THE VISIT ON CHARLES DARWIN'S DEVELOPMENT

(i) The Evolution of a Model of a Changing World

BEFORE WE CONSIDER IN DETAIL the manner in which the eight days at King George's Sound may have contributed to the development of Darwin's ideas, it may be helpful to consider how his 'world view' was changing during the voyage, particularly its last few months.

When Darwin embarked on the *Beagle*, his philosophical views were those typical of a well-educated young Englishman. Like a number of his contemporaries from Shrewsbury School and Christ's College, he was considering entering the ordained ministry of the Church of England.[62] Such a retreat into a 'quiet parsonage' would have meant his joining a long line of 'parson naturalists' that included such distinguished names as John Ray and Gilbert White, not to mention his own friend John Stevens Henslow.

He took with him aboard ship a Greek New Testament, and he seems to have attended, and indeed enjoyed, religious services held aboard ship, both at sea and at certain ports of call. He has many positive things to say about Christian missionaries.

The conventional (but certainly not the only) view of nature in the Church of England, was that, at some not-too-remote time, God had created all plants and animals, each adapted in a most elegant way, to its environment and way of life.[63] The range of variation within a species was strictly limited. The term 'natural theology' is used to designate this doctrine. It seems that even by the time he reached Australia, he was still, in part of his mind at least, a *creationist*,[64] although he was trying to reconcile the facts that he had been accumulating for the previous four years with conventional doctrine.

> [January 19 1836, Near Walerawang, New South Wales]
> I had been lying on a sunny bank, and was reflecting on the strange character of the animals of this country as compared to the rest of the world. An unbeliever in everything beyond his own reason might exclaim, 'Surely two distinct Creators must have been at work; their object, however has been the same & certainly the end in each case is

complete'. Whilst thus thinking, I observed the conical pitfall of a Lion-Ant: a fly fell in & immediately disappeared; then came a large but unwary Ant. His struggles to escape being very violent, the little jets of sand described by Kirby (Vol. 1, p. 425) were promptly directed against him. His fate, however, was better than that of the fly's. Without doubt the predacious Larva belongs to the same genus but to a different species from the European kind. — Now what would the Disbeliever say to this? Would any two workmen ever hit on so beautiful, so simple & yet so artificial a contrivance? It cannot be thought so. The one hand has surely worked throughout the universe. A Geologist perhaps would suggest that the periods of Creation have been distinct & removed one from the other; that the Creator rested in his labor. (*Journal*)

The 'Geologist' was perhaps himself, for this idea of multiple creations recurs in the *Beagle* writings: six months later for instance, he was to write to Henslow from St Helena of that island as 'this little centre of a distinct creation'.[65]

An important influence on Charles Darwin, throughout much of the voyage was that of Lyell's *Principles of Geology* (1830-1833, 3 Vols, London: John Murray). This finely written book is subtitled: *An Attempt to Explain the Former Changes of the Earth's Surface, by Causes Now in Operation*, and is a brilliant exposition of the doctrine of uniformitarianism: this is the notion that the history of the earth can be explained in terms of the long-continued action of processes that are going on NOW. According to Lyell, the physical world was undergoing gradual but continuous change, governed by ascertainable natural laws. Darwin had found these ideas extremely useful when viewing, for example, the mountains and rivers of South America, and the volcanic islands of the Pacific: an extrapolation backwards in time of the processes he was able to observe was sufficient to account for the diversity of the planet's features. However, from late 1835 onwards, he was struck by the power of organisms to modify their environment. Particularly, of course, he was impressed by the ability of coral polyps to produce land. In October and November 1835 the *Beagle* made her long passage from the Galapagos to Tahiti.

We passed through the Low or Dangerous Archipelago, and saw several of those curious rings of coral land, just rising above the water's edge, which have been called Lagoon Islands. A long and brilliantly white beach is capped by a margin of green vegetation; and the strip, looking either way, rapidly narrows away in the distance and sinks beneath the horizon. From the mast head a wide expanse of smooth water can be seen within the ring. These low coral islands bear no proportion to the vast ocean out of which they abruptly rise; and it seems wonderful that such weak invaders are not overwhelmed, by the all-powerful and never tiring waves of the great sea, miscalled the Pacific. (*Voyage*)

An intensive period of survey in Tahiti followed, and by the end of the year, before he had arrived in Australia, he had prepared the first draft of his paper on the origin of coral islands. In this he set forth his idea that fringing and barrier coral reefs and atolls are successive members of a series formed as the result of rising sea levels or subsidence of islands. In other words, in relation to island environments at least, *organisms were able to effect changes in the physical environment.* Howard Gruber[66] has set out his model of the changes that occurred in Darwin's world view in a series of diagrams, reproduced here in Figure 23.

Another notion that Darwin must have come across in reading Lyell, perhaps during that long passage across the Pacific after the *Beagle*'s visit to the Galapagos Islands, was the possibility of the mutability of species, the concept that grew into the *Origin of Species by Means of Natural Selection*, in 1959. Lyell, in his first edition (1830-1833), is exceedingly cautious, but appears to come close to admitting the possibility of the mutability of species. We know that Charles had the second volume of Lyell's *Principles* in his cabin when he visited the Galapagos and the Pacific coral islands. In that volume appear the following passages:

> Having shown in the last chapter how considerably the numerical increase or the extension of the geographical range of one species must derange the numbers and distributions of others, let us now direct our attention to the influence which inorganic causes described in our first volume are continually exerting on the habitations of species.
>
> No sooner had a volcanic isle been thrown up than some lichens begin to grow upon it, and it is sometimes clothed with verdure while smoke and ashes are still occasionally thrown from the crater. The cocoa, pandanus and mangrove take root upon the coral reef before it has fairly risen above the waves.
>
> Every flood and landslip, every wave which a hurricane or earthquake throws against the shore, every shower of volcanic dust and ashes which buries a country far and wide to the depth of many feet, every advance of the sand-flood, every conversion of salt-water into fresh when rivers alter their main channel of drainage, every permanent variation in the rise or fall of tides in an estuary—these and countless other causes displace in the course of a few centuries certain plants and animals from the stations they previously occupied. (p. 158)
>
> Species . . . are, in general, local, some being confined to extremely small spots . . . Hence it must happen that when the nature of these localities is changed, the species will perish. (p. 166)
>
> If the reader should infer, from the facts laid before him in the proceeding chapters, that successive extinctions of animals and plants

may be part of the regular course of nature, he will naturally inquire whether there are any means provided for the repair of these losses? ... is it possible that new species can be called into being from time to time, and yet so astonishing a phenomenon can escape the attention of naturalists?

> [By a critical study of biologically rich regions and of recent geological formations] ... we may learn which of the species now our contemporaries ... have made their appearance when the animate world had nearly attained its present conditions.
>
> From such data we may be enabled to infer whether species have been called into existence in succession or all at one period; whether singly or by groups simultaneously; whether the antiquity of man be as high as of any inferior beings which now share the planet with him, or whether the human species is one of the most recent. (p. 179)

Yet Lyell seems ambivalent, and his caution intermittently shines through,

> It is idle to dispute about the abstract possibility of the conversion of one species to another, when there are known causes so much more active in their nature, which must always intervene and prevent the accomplishment of such conversions. (p. 174)

Although Darwin seems, *at this time*, to have entrusted none of his ideas on the mutability of species to paper, with Lyell's tentative notions hammering at the back of his mind, the *possibility* that one species of organism might, in due time, change into another, must surely have occurred to him as he explored the islands of the Pacific he encountered and the entirely novel plants and animals of *Terra Australis* (see again the quotation of p. 51).

The association with islands is perhaps worth stressing, for it also links Darwin's field-work in the Galapagos, the Western Pacific (which he visited *before* arriving in Australia) with his studies in the Cocos (Keeling) Group (which he undertook *after* leaving Western Australia). Concerning the Keelings, he wrote to his sister Caroline:

> I am very glad we called there ... The subject of coral formation has for the last half year been a point of particular interest to me. I hope to be able to put some of the facts in a more simple and connected point of view than they have hitherto been considered. The idea of a lagoon island 30 miles in diameter being based on a submarine crater of equal dimensions has always appeared to me a monstrous hypothesis. (29 April 1836, CULM/DAR 223)

All these studies were probably undertaken with Lyell's uniformitarian ideas, including the possibility of a 'succession' of species, in his mind.

Many of the quotations from the *Principles* on pages 53 and 54 relate specifically to the volcanic island, coral reef and sea-shore environments that Darwin was encountering in the Pacific and Indian Oceans.

Further evidence that Darwin's ideas on islands were closely interwoven with the notion of the mutability of species, and that he was to some extent indebted to Lyell for both, is apparent, in his paper on coral atolls. In this paper, presented to the meeting of the Geological Society of London of 31 May 1837 (nine months after his return and some three months after his 'insight' with regard to the transmutability of species[67]) he advanced the theory that atolls were formed by the subsidence of volcanic masses. Amongst the results of this hypothesis were the following:

> ... That certain coral formations acting as monuments over subsided land, the geographical distribution of organic beings (as consequent on geological changes as laid down by Mr Lyell) is elucidated, by the discovery of **former centres whence the germs could be disseminated.**

and

> ... That some degree of light thus be thrown on the question, whether certain groups of living beings peculiar to some spots are the remnants of a former large population, or **a new one springing into existence.**[68] (Emphasis not in original)

There exists the possibility, therefore, that ideas on environmental change, and the possibility that this might be associated with species change, were at least at the back of Darwin's mind as he explored the shores and bushland around King George's Sound in March 1836. What evidence is there that this work influenced or was influenced by his observations in Western Australia?

In looking through Darwin's notes, both his more finished *Geological Diary*, and his rough preliminary annotations (see Chapter 1) one cannot fail to be impressed by the amount of cross-referencing between the accounts of the Pacific Islands, King George's Sound and Keeling. There are frequent marginal notes linking these sets of observations; many of them dating from the period of the voyage. Darwin, during sea passages perhaps, must have gone through his notes, comparing one site with another, and his observations on the plants and animals of one locality with those elsewhere. A couple of examples must suffice; in his description of the Bald Head site, written up in March 1836, he expressed himself a little puzzled about the origin of so much calcareous, sandy material:

> ... it must be asked, where will a sea coast be found near which pure calcareous powder drifted about, in a like manner as sand in ordinary sand dunes? I can give no answer to this ...

A marginal note (a) directs the reader to a note on the back of the sheet, dated April 1836:

> The sand on the shores of the Lagoon Island of Keeling is entirely calcareous. — I could not discover in the sand a particle otherwise constituted. But there was this difference that all the particles had served at one time as parts of living animals, whereas here the matter must have been a calcareous powder . . .

Elsewhere in the geological notes on Western Australia,[69] Darwin has hurriedly scribbled some notes, apparently partly based on his own observations:

> Rev. Capt. King Lagoon in [B?*illegible*] reef.
> From the presence of some Tertiary formations and shells at [?*illegible*], recent elevation on SW & W extremity of New Holland. — Put in Coral Paper & References about E. Indies & Archipelago.
> The Monument of Lagoon Is?
> Quote extent of formation & rise in land, calcareous part, not noticed in Europe.

Cryptic indeed though these scrappy annotations are, the 'Put in Coral Paper' as well as the phrase 'The Monument of Lagoon Is'[70] and the references to reefs, all serve to link his King George's Sound notes with his Coral Island writings.

There are also hints in his geological notes that he thought that elevation of the land had affected the Sound. This is significant, as not many months previously he had been working on the west coast of South America, and had become convinced that the 'Roads of Coquimbo' (described by Lyell in *Principles*) in Chile were the result of marine action's cutting of beaches high above the present level of the sea, and thus that continental elevation on a substantial scale had taken place. (He presented these ideas to the Geological Society of London not long after his return to England.[71]) Moreover, a part of his coral atoll theory was the notion that 'both in the Pacific and Indian Oceans . . . spaces of great extent are undergoing movements . . . and that bands of elevation and subsidence alternate'.[72] He felt certain (probably incorrectly) that the Bald Head deposits, accumulating far up the sides of the 600 ft ridge had formed when the land had 'stood lower'.[73]

In his notes on Coral islands in the CULM/DAR 41 folio (the pages are unnumbered), is a set of 23 pages of observations, illustrated by diagrams, on the coral beaches and atolls of Tahiti. On the back of a page of notes on sediment accumulation is a pencilled 'We know that sediment at King George's Sound will accumulate at (30°)', an observation based on the false bedding at Bald Head.

We may in addition note that the possible association between King George's Sound and coral features must have been in Darwin's mind before he even went ashore: in the *Voyage of the Beagle* he relates how he accompanied Captain FitzRoy to Bald Head, 'the place mentioned by so many navigators, where some imagined they saw corals, and others petrified trees.' Darwin had evidently been doing the background reading necessary before the fieldwork commenced!

Howard Gruber has suggested that during the period 1832 to 1837 Darwin's view of the world had changed from the stable model given in Figure 23A (p. 50), to the more dynamic view of Figure 23D. The adoption of this posture, was gradual, and may only have been completed after Charles' return to England, but his studies of the dynamic nature of coral coastlines may have accelerated the change: any such evolution of his outlook would have received a good deal of reinforcement from Volume II of Lyell's *Principles*.

It is tempting to surmise that Darwin's study of the Bald Head site, with its abundance of 'fossils', and the picture it evoked in his mind of an accumulated mass of wind-blown sand overwhelming the bushes and trees as they struggled to grow through it, contributed to the development of the concept of an animal and plant community both responding to, and influencing a changing physical environment. Alas it is impossible to demonstrate this with certainty, although the effort put into studying and recording the site was substantial, and the links with his writings on the dynamic nature of coral environments are extensive. Figure 24 attempts to show some of the interrelationships amongst the ideas forming in Darwin's mind during latter stages of the *Beagle* voyage, and some of the stimuli that may have influenced their development.

58

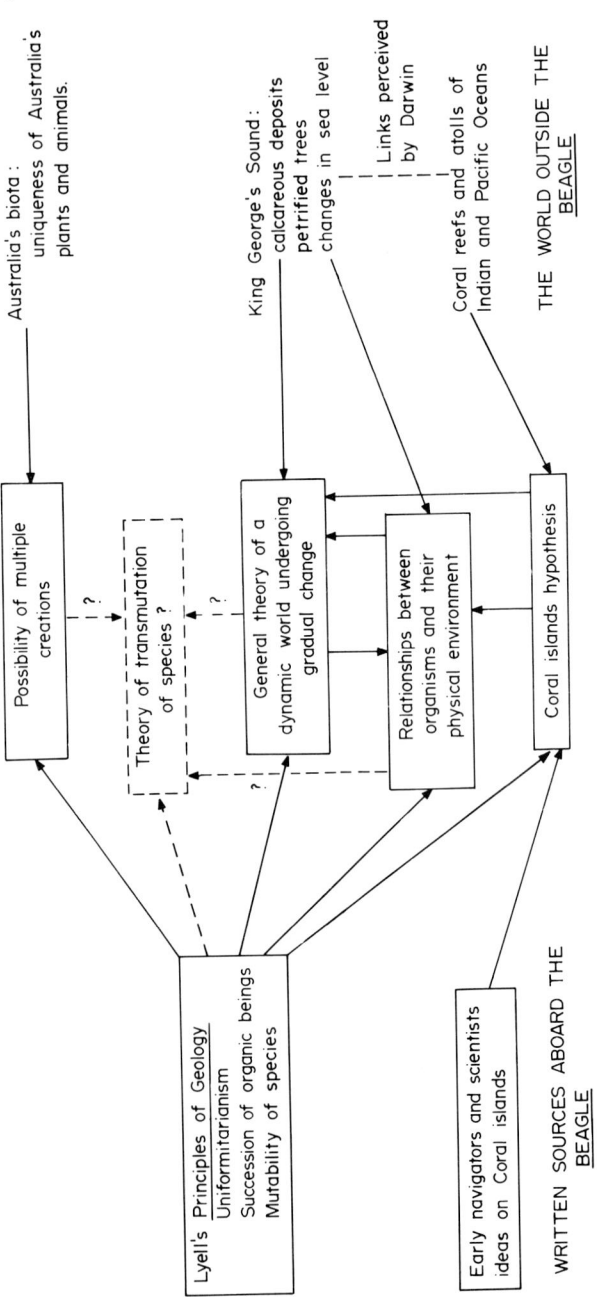

Figure 24—Darwin's ideas during the last months of the *Beagle*'s voyage. Darwin was influenced both by the printed sources available to him, such as Lyell, and the environments in Australia and the Indo-Pacific he experienced. These stimuli contributed to the development of a number of ideas, between which links existed. See also Figure 23.

Chapter 6

THE EFFECT OF THE VISIT ON CHARLES DARWIN'S DEVELOPMENT:

(ii) Strange Beings of an Isolated Continent

TO SOME EXTENT Darwin's experiences in Western Australia simply extended and complemented his journeys in New South Wales and Tasmania. The strangeness, to him, of the plants and animals he encountered as he wandered through the bush is readily conveyed to the readers of the *Voyage of the Beagle* by the perceptive young English naturalist:

> The extreme uniformity of the vegetation is the most remarkable feature of the landscape of the greater part of New South Wales. Everywhere we have open woodland, the ground covered with a very thin pasture, with little appearance of verdure. The trees nearly all belong to one family and mostly have their leaves placed in a vertical, instead of, as in Europe, in a nearly horizontal position: the foliage is scanty, and of a peculiar pale green tint, without any gloss ... The leaves are not shed periodically ...
>
> The greater number of the trees ... do not attain a large size, but they grow tall and tolerably straight, and stand well apart. The bark of some of the Eucalypti falls annually, or hangs dead in long shreds which swing about with the wind, and give the woods a desolate and untidy appearance. I cannot imagine a more complete contrast, in every respect, than between the forests of Valdivia or Chiloe, and the woods of Australia. (*Voyage*, near Emu Ferry, New South Wales, 16 January 1836)

Besides the eucalypts, which obviously impressed him, Darwin collected kangaroo-rats and a duck-billed platypus, he saw cockatoos and parrots, and he makes frequent mention in his writings of emus and kangaroos. He noted too, that the insects[74] and molluscs were different. The individuality and uniqueness of Australia was clear enough to him in the field, but it must have been confirmed as he examined, in co-operation with such specialists as Jenyns, Gould, Waterhouse, Bell and Henslow[75] the insects, molluscs, mammals, fish and other specimens taken back to England.

Specimens were collected in large numbers from all of the three Australian colonies he visited, and it was clear to Darwin, as it was clear to many other naturalists, that this uniqueness was the product of long isolation, as much as of any individuality of the Australian environment. He noted the way in which the absence of placental mammals was compensated for by the existence of marsupials that, in some classes at least, had a similar way of life to certain placentals elsewhere. Moreover, he discovered through the written works of William Clift[76] that the distinctiveness of Australia's mammal fauna had also existed in the past.

In the *Origin of Species*, and in the various writings preparatory to it, Darwin makes frequent reference to the evidence provided by geographical distributions, for example, in the *Essay of 1844*.[77]

> I think that I am justified in asserting that most of the above ... points in geographical distribution of past and present organisms ... follow as a consequence of specific forms being mutable and of their being adapted by natural selection to diverse ends, conjoined with their powers of dispersal, and the geologico-geographical changes now in slow progress and which have undoubtedly taken place. This large class of facts being thus explained, far more than counterbalances many separate difficulties and apparent objections in convincing my mind of the truth of this theory of common descent.

In the transmutation notebooks, begun early in 1837, and in which Darwin noted, usually in a highly abbreviated form, ideas and references that assisted him in building his 'species theory', there are a number of notes that showed that he believed that the phenomenon of isolation was closely associated with the development of new species. Besides references to island environments such as the Galapagos, there are no fewer than 92 uses of the words 'Australia', 'Australian' and 'Australians'. He saw Australia as the isolated 'island continent'.

The same theme is found in the *Sketch of 1842*,[78] which Darwin referred to later as 'the first very brief abstract of my theory', originally 35 pages of pencil notes, written in June of that year. For example:

> Change of external conditions, and isolation either by chance landing of a form on an island, or subsidence dividing a continent, or a great chain of mountains and the number of individuals not being numerous, will best favour variation and selection.

In the *Essay of 1844*, a much longer expression of his views that is found in the *Sketch*, Darwin again draws attention to Australia's isolation and distinctiveness, particularly in her mammalian fauna.

> It is well known that all mammifers (as well as all other organisms) are united in one great system; but that the different species, genera, or

families of the same order inhabit different quarters of the globe. If we divided the land into two divisions according to the amount of difference ... of the terrestrial mammifers inhabiting them, we shall have first Australia including New Guinea, and secondly the rest of the world.

He felt it was far more reasonable to explain these patterns of geographical distribution by assuming common ancestry, followed by later separation, isolation and evolutionary development than to assume that a Creator, would time and time again, create two or more different organisms that were distinct, but belonging to the same major group.

A comparison with the Galapagos is perhaps worthwhile. Darwin noted in that Pacific Island group:

1. That the organisms on each island were different; they had therefore been isolated from each other for some time.
2. Yet, there was sufficient similarity for him to assume a common ancestor in the remote past.
3. Moreover, the organisms of the archipelago were of such a character for it to be possible to assume that their ancestors had arrived from elsewhere: thus although mammals, that would have difficulty in making the journey were absent, the birds that were present had American affinities.[79]

It was paradoxically not only the *individuality* and *uniqueness* of island (and other isolated) organisms, but also their *similarity* to creatures elsewhere that provided Darwin with confirmation of his theory of the transmutability of species. The idea of *representation* — the notion that one species 'represented' another related form in a distant area was an important one for Darwin.

He seems to have thought of the differences between the plants of Western Australia and the eastern colonies in these terms. In his *Notebook D* Charles wrote in 1838 'In Australia plants E & W very different'. In writing this he may have been in part recalling his own impressions, but his observations of the plants around King George's Sound do not seem to have been very extensive. He did however, in the *Voyage*, comment on the apparent differences in the abundance of *Casuarina* and *Eucalyptus* trees, as compared to parts of eastern Australia with which he was familiar, and also on the grass trees (*Xanthorrhoea*) which forms such a striking element of the flora of southwestern Australia. If he did discern, at the time of his visit, any important differences between the bush of New South Wales and Tasmania (where he had been struck by the giant tree-ferns) on the one hand and King George's Sound on the other, he may already have been alerted to look out for it by Lyell, who, in Volume II of the *Principles*, published in 1832, not only mentioned the difference, but had an explanation for it. Bearing in mind how little the flora and geography of Australia were then known, the following passage is extraordinarily prescient:

> If when this continent has been more thoroughly investigated, we do not discover some physical barriers, such as a great lake, or a desert, or a lofty mountain range intervening between these districts, there may perhaps be geological evidence hereafter discovered, that a sea was interspersed up to a recent period, separating two large islands. (*Principles*, Vol. II, p. 174)

Darwin returned again and again, in the writings that led up to the *Origin*, to the significance of the contrasts, and yet also the similarities, in the biota of Western and Eastern Australia.

> We may clearly observe, as in the main divisions of the world, that sub-barriers divide differeng groups of species, although the opposite sides of such sub-barriers may possess nearly the same climate, and may in other respects be nearly similar ... Deserts, arms of the sea, and even rivers form the barriers; mere pre-occupied space seems sufficient ... thus Eastern and Western Australia, in the same latitude, with very similar climate and soils, have scarcely a plant, and few animals or birds in common, although all belong to the peculiar genera characterising Australia. It is in short impossible to explain the differences in the inhabitants, either of the main divisions of the world, or of these sub-divisions by differences in their physical conditions, and by the adaptation of their inhabitants. Some other cause must intervene. (*Essay of 1844*, p. 174)

In order to trace the influence of Western Australia on Darwin's ideas a little further, we must now introduce a new actor in the drama: Joseph Hooker. Hooker's background was remarkably similar to that of Darwin: at the age of twenty-two, the same age that Charles had embarked on the *Beagle*, after a medical training, he had sailed with Captain Ross, as naturalist on the *Erebus*, and voyaged to the Antarctic. He had very briefly met Darwin (while walking through Trafalgar Square), and he had received an advance copy of the *Voyage of the Beagle* (via Lyell, to whom Darwin had sent a set of proofs). On his return, three years later from southern parts (where he had visited Australia and New Zealand), Joseph Hooker worked on the plants Charles had brought back from the Galapagos, and upon his own *Flora of New Zealand*, *Flora of Tasmania* and *Flora Antarctica*, and there blossomed, if one may use such a word for an association between the two naturalists, a friendship that was to prove lifelong. Darwin wrote to Hooker on 11 January 1844:

> Besides a general interest about the southern lands, I have been now ever since my return engaged in presumptuous work & which I know

no one individual would not say a very foolish one ... I have never ceased collecting facts—at least the gleams of light have come, & I am convinced (quite contrary to the opinion I started with) that species are not (it is like confessing to a murder) immutable ... I think I have found out (here's presumption!) the simple way by which species became exquisitely adapted to various ends.

The friendship developed almost into scientific co-operation; Darwin and Hooker met several times during 1844, in London and at Down House, Kent, where Charles and his bride (and cousin) Emma (née Wedgwood) were now living.[80] Joseph Hooker read through the *Essay of 1844* (he thought portions 'goodish' according to Charles own marginal annotations), and he acknowledged freely the assistance that Charles gave to his own botanical work on southern hemisphere floras and their relationship to the 'species theory', while they were sitting in the Old Study at Down, or walking round the Sandwalk, Charles' 'Thinking Walk', that encircled a strip of land of 1.5 acres, that he had planted out as a copse.

Another particular focus of these discussions will have been the striking difference between the plants of Western Australia and those of the eastern side of the continent. Joseph Hooker makes a very great deal of this in his *Flora of Tasmania*, as the following quotations illustrate:

> As far as I can make out, about one fifth of the south-eastern species are found beyond that area; but only one tenth in south-western Australia ...

> What differences there are in conditions would ... favour the idea that south-eastern Australia, from its greater area, many large rivers, extensive tracts of mountainous country and humid forests would present the most extensive Flora, of which only the drier types could extend into south-western Australia. But such is not the case altogether, for though the far greater area is much the best explored, presents more varied conditions, and is tenanted by a larger number of Natural Orders, these contain fewer species by many hundreds.

> Of the largest genera in south-eastern and south-western Australia there are very few species common to both countries, as the following list will show. (p. li)

Then there follows an elaborate statistical table showing the botanical dissimilarities between the two sides of the continent.

Darwin's own annotations in his copy of the *Flora of Tasmania* (inscribed 'C Darwin, from the author') are interesting and important. He vigorously double-scored in the margin alongside the first sentence quoted above, inserted the phrase 'Eyre's desert between' against the second and the single word 'wonderful' by the last.

A few pages later in the same volume Hooker continues:

> The local character of the south-western Australian plants in another singular feature that must not be over-looked in an inquiry as to the relative ages of countries and their vegetation . . . the species of Swan River differ very much from King George's Sound. I am quite at a loss to offer any possible reason for this . . . the contrast in this respect is all the more remarkable, because the latter also, compared with other parts of the world, presents a very considerable assemblage of local species. But so it is that there are far more King George's Sound species absent from the Swan River, though separated by only 200 miles of tolerably level land, than there are Tasmanian plants absent from Victoria, which are as many miles apart and separated by an oceanic strait . . . As this excessive multiplication must, under the theory of creation by variation, have occupied a great length of time, it seems . . . natural to assume on purely botanical grounds, that Western Australian Flora is the earliest, and sent colonists to the eastern quarter, where they became mixed with Indian, Polynesian etc., colonists, than the western Flora was peopled by one section of the inhabitants of the eastern quarter. (p. liv)

Again the last sentence is heavily double-scored in the margin by Darwin, and annotated 'Was not S W Corner an archipelago with representative species like Galapagos . . .???' Although as far as I know Darwin never published this suggestion, it has subsequently been quite independently advanced, by other West Australian botanists such as Churchill.[81] Darwin had, as he thought, the evidence of his own eyes, in the shape of the ferruginous sandstone, and some of the calcareous sediments at King George's Sound that 'the land has stood lower in relation to the sea' (Chapter 5). The fact that this suggestion, like of course, a number of others of Darwin, does not achieve unanimous support today does not detract from the significance of that tiny, pencilled marginal comment. Many years after he had said 'Farewell' to Western Australia 'without sorrow or regret', Darwin was regarding Australia in general, and Western Australia in particular, with its complexities of isolation, as the 'Galapagos writ large'.

Many Darwinian scholars have attempted to show that a particular visit, personal association or idea was especially significant in the development of Charles Darwin's work. He himself thought his association with Henslow while at Cambridge, his visit to the Galapagos, and then, late in 1838, his reading of Malthus' *Essay on Population* were particularly significant. And he had the very greatest respect for Joseph Hooker, for in instructions prepared for Emma, Charles suggested that he would be 'quite the best person' to edit and prepare his 'Species Book' for the press, in the event of his own early death.

But in reality no one incident or individual can be said to be paramount. His voracious mind chewed through a mass of geological, biological and anthropological material, read in the short years between his return from the sea, in October 1836 and the completion of the *Essay* in the summer of 1844. He had a multitude of exciting experiences during the *Beagle* voyage. And before, and after, the voyage (and even to some extent during it, through his correspondence with Henslow, who received his specimens, and published some of his first findings) he was a node in an important network of human relationships that were valuable to him. Thus two of his scientific colleagues, Jenyns and Hooker, were related by marriage to his friend and teacher, Professor Henslow. The views of Lyell pressed mightily on him from the *Principles*, even as he worked on his notes and *Journal* in the cabin of the *Beagle*; the published diary in the form of the *Voyage*, then reached Joseph Hooker, via Lyell, just as Joseph was preparing to go on his own voyage of discovery. Hooker, then, embracing some of Darwin's early thoughts on evolution, and sharpening them in the light of his own experiences in Australasia and elsewhere, was a powerful influence back on the more mature Darwin . . . and so on.

Charles Darwin's visit to King George's Sound, one of his three encounters with Australian environments, came *after* his visits to South America and the Galapagos, and the writing of the first draft of the coral paper, but *before* the completion of his work on coral, his visits to the remote islands of Ascension, Mauritius and St Helena, and the frantic period of sorting, discussion and writing as a member of the circle of the leading scientific men in England in the period after late 1836. We can detect the influence of the Australian interlude, in lesser or greater degree in Darwin's work on coral reefs, on the transmutability of species, on humankind, as well as on plants and animals and their distributions. Darwin's time in Tasmania and New South Wales has not yet been subjected to the thorough scrutiny it warrants, but I hope I have demonstrated in this short essay on the naturalist's West Australian experience that Australia was a significant image in the brilliant stream of consciousness, all of which, directly or indirectly, led to the development of the greatest polymath mind of the nineteenth century. Slender thread though it was, its distinctive hue, although often mixed with fibres of other colours, can be detected in the bright fabric of Charles Darwin's 45 years of writing.

APPENDIX

Australia, the Red Notebook, and the Transmutation Theory

IN EDITING CHARLES DARWIN's *Red Notebook*,[82] Sandra Herbert wrote that 'it stands at the beginning of the chain of events which led from Darwin's assertion of a belief in the mutability of species through his arrival at the notion of natural selection and then, after twenty years and by way of several drafts, to the publication in 1859 of the *Origin of Species*'. The *Red Notebook* contains, in the pages following page 130, the first known writings by Darwin on the mutability of species — written in about March 1837, after H.M.S. *Beagle* had returned to England. The notebook also contains geological, oceanographical, botanical and zoological entries and thus encapsulates Darwin's many-sided genius. It spans the final few months of the *Beagle*'s voyage and the entry of the young Darwin into the company of some of England's most brilliant scientists in London in late 1836 and early 1837. It also is transitional in another sense, linking as it does his field notebooks (some eighteen of them) and his other descriptive annotations made on the voyage, and the more specialised, theoretical notebooks (A, B, C, D, E, M and N) dealing with geology and the 'species theory'.

The book itself is a small (164 mm × 99 mm), somewhat faded, leather-bound notebook, with 90 leaves. Many of the pages were removed by Darwin, and kept with other notes. Most, but not all, of the excised pages have come to light in the Darwin Archives of the Cambridge University Library, where the *Red Notebook* is now held. It contains some field observations, but also ideas, references and notes for papers he planned to write. The first 110 pages or so yield, as Mrs Herbert puts it, 'a perfect progression of place names corresponding to points visited by the *Beagle* from late May to the end of September 1836'. On this basis she dates the opening of the notebook to 'May or June 1836'. Her diagram showing the chronological relationship of Darwin's various notebooks seems to indicate that she feels mid-June to be the most likely moment.

I believe, however, that if the *topics* covered by the entries in the first few pages of the notebook are considered, and compared with contempor-

ary Darwinian writings (his *Geological* and *Zoological Diaries* from the *Beagle*), a rather earlier date is indicated.
   Almost every item in the first nine extant pages of the notebook (i.e. pp. 5-12, and 15; pp. 1-4, 13 and 14 are missing) echoes one of the themes that Darwin must have been thinking about in the days immediately following his departure from King George's Sound on 14 March 1836, as he wrote up and reviewed his notes on the *Beagle*'s eight-day sojourn there, and read what he could concerning the phenomena he has observed in Western Australia in the quite extensive library he had with him on the *Beagle*. I very briefly summarise these correspondences below:

> The first paragraph on the first known pages runs:
>
> La.billardière mentions the floating marine Confervae, is very common within E. Indian Archipelago, no minute description, calls it a Fucus. P. [Vol. 1, p. 287].

Sandra Herbert points out that Jacques Julien Houton de Labillardière's *Relation du voyage à la recherche de La Pérouse ... 1791-1792* (Paris, 1800), Vol. 1, p. 287, reads:

> Je revis le fucus que j'avois auparavant recontré tout près de la Nouvelle-Guinée; il ressemble à de l'étoupe très-fine coupée par petis morceaux longs d'environ trois centimètres: ce sont des filamens aussi fins que des cheveux. On les voyoit souvent réunis en faisceaux, et si nombreux qu'ils ternissoient l'eau de la rade.

The incident that triggered Darwin's reference to Labillardière's account was almost certainly that described on page 29, the *Beagle*'s passing through an area where the sea was covered with what would now presumably be described as phytoplankton.
   The latter part of page 5, page 6 and page 7 of the notebook include the following entries:

> P. 379. Henslow Anglesea, nodules in Clay Slate, major axis 2½ ft – singular structure of nodule, constitution [same as] of slate same – longer axis in line of Cleavage. laminae fold round them; Quote this. Valparaiso Granitic nodules in Gneiss.
>
> Epidote seems commonly to occur where rocks have undergone action of heat. It is so found in Anglesea, amongst the varying & dubious granites – Wide limits of this mineral in Australia. Fritton's appendix.
>
> Carbonate of Lime disseminated through the great Plas Newydd dike – Mem. tres. Montes. [Henslow Anglesea.]
>   great variety in nature of a dike. – Mem. at Chronos & Conception p. 417.

Veins of quartz exceedingly rare Mem. C. [Cape] Turn p. 434 & 419.
As limestone passes into schist scales of chlorites — Mem Maldonado p. 375
Much Chlorite in some of the dikes —
p. 432 as in Andes.

All the page references in the above have been identified as being to Professor John Stevens Henslow's 'Geological Description at Anglesea', which was published in the *Transactions of the Cambridge Philosophical Society*, Vol. 1, pp. 359–452, 1821–2.

In almost every case some reference to the phenomena mentioned above can be found in Darwin's geological notes of the King George's Sound area. Granite and Gneiss rock-types, the gradation of one rock-type into another, cleavage, dykes, veins — all these were encountered by Charles in his few days of fieldwork in Western Australia (see, for example, the quotations on pp. 22, 23 and 26).

In view of these strong correspondences one is left with the impression that Darwin, shortly after examining the igneous and metamorphic rocks of King George's Sound, read what he could about similar phenomena elsewhere. He had aboard the *Beagle* a copy of the paper on Anglesea by his friend, John Henslow, in which very similar features were described. Points that interested him were noted down together with brief reminders of where he had seen such things earlier in his travels.

The reference 'Fritton's appendix' (p. 6 of the notebook) confirms this general picture. This refers to an appendix by William Fritton on 'Geology' in Captain Phillip P. King's *Narrative of a Survey of Intertropical and Western Coasts of Australia Performed Between the Years 1818 and 1822* (London 1827), a copy of which was also in the cabin of the *Beagle*, and used frequently by Darwin and Captain FitzRoy ... For example in the *Geological Diary* (DAR. 38.1/867) Darwin compares a fine-grained, ferruginous sandstone encountered at King George's Sound with one described by Dr Fritton.

The first part of page 8 of the notebook reads:

> In Dampier's voyage there is a mine of meteorology with respect to the discussion of winds and storms.

On the two succeeding pages there are a number of references to Dampier's descriptions of the seas off the West Coast of 'New Holland'. The volume involved here (again identified by Herbert) is William Dampier's *A New Voyage Round the World*, especially part 3: *A Discourse of Trade-Winds, Breezes, Storms, Seasons of the Year, Tides and Currents of the Torrid Zone* ... (1699).

It would seem quite probable that Darwin would refer to this work during the passage from King George's Sound to the Cocos Islands – off the coasts of Western Australia that Dampier describes in considerable detail. The supposition that he might turn to an account of '... Trade-winds, Breezes, Storms ... Tides and Currents' is perhaps given strength when one knows from the meteorological record of the ship that at 6 a.m. on 16 March 1836, the vessel 'passed through a remarkable tide ripple or meeting of waters', and that according to one of Charles Darwin's letters, 'gales and foul weather' were experienced later in the passage – 27 March onwards.

On page 12 of the *Red Notebook*, Darwin returns to geological matters and refers again to the French explorer:

> M. La.billardière in Bay of Legrand, (SW part) describes a Small granite isld capped by Calcareous rock; following ... (note incomplete as p. 13 was excised and has not been located).

Several times, in his own geological notes, Darwin was at pains to point out the relationship between the granites and the overlying sedimentary rocks – limestones and sandstones of the King George's Sound area:

> The granitic formation is everywhere in the low country smoothed over by sedimentary deposits. (DAR. 38.1/866)

> ... ferruginous and calcareous matter and minute particles of quartz were spread over the bottom of the sea and encased the ... ridges of granite ... Michaelmas Is ... according to Flinders is granite capped with calcareous layers ... (DAR 38.1/872-3)

It seems that in reading what he could about the Geology of southwestern Australia during the writing up of the fair copy of his *Geological Diary*, Darwin encountered, in Labillardière's account, a similar relationship elsewhere on the same coast.

There are so many correspondences between the first few pages of the *Red Notebook* and the Zoological and Geological notes known to have been written during or immediately following the visit to Western Australia, that one is tempted to say they were approximately contemporaneous. We know that Darwin often wrote up his *Geological Diary* and *Journal* from preliminary notes, and it is reasonable to assume that he did this shortly after the observations described, when he had the necessary leisure. The passage to Keeling would have provided such an opportunity. Almost every item in the first few extant pages of the *Red Notebook* touches either on that sector of the Voyage, or upon the immediately preceding few days at the Sound. The first remaining item in the book can tentatively be dated about 18 March 1836 (the date of the confervae notes). On this basis I very tentatively assign the opening of the notebook to within a few days of Charles Darwin's departure from Australia. If a piece of complete speculation were to be allowed, I would expect that should the missing pages 1-4 of the Notebook ever appear, they might hold a reference to the site in Western Australia that was of most interest to Darwin — Bald Head!

Why the visit to Western Australia should trigger the slight but appreciable change in Darwin's method of working that the opening of the *Red Notebook* implies is also a matter for speculation. But possibly having glimpsed the strange plants and animals of this isolated continent, following so shortly after his portentous visit to the Galapagos, he sensed that an important part of his observation, collecting and recording was complete, and the time for analysis, thought, conjecture and hypothesis was at hand. By early 1836 it seems likely that the transformation in his word view symbolised in Figure 23 was not quite complete, but was well underway.

We have seen that there are very few hints in Charles Darwin's *Beagle* writings, before, during or subsequent to his Australian sojourn, to indicate that he was entertaining ideas concerning the transmutability of species. Yet the analogy between the Galapagos and Australia, the importance of isolation as a factor in evolution in his later writings, and the *Red Notebook*, possibly opened within sight of Western Australia, and containing, written after his return to England his first sketchy jottings on species change, all form points of contact. And Darwin had read his own Grandfather's *Zoonomia*, and Lamarck's writings on change, as well as having Lyell's *Principles* in his cabin. It is difficult to see how, faced with the kaleidoscope to which he was exposed, that the idea of transmutability could not have flickered on the edge of his mind during those last few months as Ship's Naturalist on the *Beagle*. Could it be that he was so frightened of the idea that he was afraid to entrust it to paper? (We detect a similar reticence in 1844, in his letter to Joseph Hooker, p. 63). There is one further very slight piece of circumstantial evidence that hints that this might have been so: ironically the incident connects with both the *Red Notebook* and Lyell's *Principles*.

In the first place the notebook contains many references to Lyell: there must have been frequent occasions when both were open together on the chart-table. Further, on page 32, there occurs a reference to Sir John Herschel, the distinguished English scientist and man of letters, with whom Charles spent some time while in Cape Town (31 May-18 June 1836). Darwin found his discussions with Sir John immensely stimulating: one reason for this may have been that they discussed the transmutability of species. There is no direct evidence of this, but the following facts are suggestive:

(i) In 1835 Lyell had sent a copy of the fourth edition of *Principles* to Sir John Herschel.
(ii) On 20 February 1836 Sir John wrote to thank him, describing his book

as 'one of those productions which work a complete revolution in their subject by altering entirely the point of view in which it must thence forward be contemplated'. His remarks amounted to a eulogy. He went on:

> You have succeeded, too, in adding dignity to a subject already grand by exposing to view the immense extent of the problem it offers for solution and by unveiling a dim glimpse of speculation connected with it ... where it seems impossible to venture without experiencing some degree of that mysterious awe which the sybil appeals to, in the bosom of Aeneas, on entering the confines of the shades — or what the Maid of Avenel suggests to Halbert Glendenning, 'He that on such a quest would go, must know no fear of failing; to coward soul or faithless heart the search were unavailing'. Of course I allude to that mystery of mysteries the replacement of extinct species by others. Many will doubtless think your speculations too bold — but it is as well to face the difficulty at once. For my part I cannot but think it an inadequate conception of the Creator to assume it as granted that his combinations are exhausted upon any area of the earth of their former exercise, though in this as in all his other works, we are led by all analogy to suppose that he works through a series of intermediate causes & that in consequences, the origination of fresh species, could it every come under our cognizance, would be found to be a natural in contradistinction to a miraculous process. (American Philosophical Society MSS, reproduced in L. G. Wilson, *Charles Lyell: The Years to 1841.* New Haven and London, Yale University Press, 1972.)

Clearly the book had made an immense impression on Herschel, particularly the sections dealing with the 'succession of species', and Herschel appears to be almost a transmutationist.[83]

(iii) Darwin, of course, also had with him a copy of the *Principles*, and had been reading it in the weeks, possibly even the days before H.M.S. *Beagle* berthed in Cape Town on 31 May 1836, just three months after Herschel's letter to Lyell.

It would scarcely be surprising if the two scientists (Herschel and Darwin), having such similar interests, should have found some common ground in the transmutability of species as they sat over their wine, after dining together in Cape Town in June 1836. Yet the *Red Notebook* is silent on this. Such was the diffidence with which the young Darwin treated the notion, that we may never be certain.

Notes

1. The date of Charles Darwin's entry to school and brief particulars of his contemporaries can be established from *Shrewsbury School Register*, edited by J. E. Auden; Wordall, Mishall and Thomas, Oswestry, 1909.
2. The long association is documented in: *Darwin and Henslow: the Growth of an Idea: Letters 1831–1860*, edited by Nora Barlow; Bentham-Moxon Trust and John Murray, London, 1967. It is perhaps worth mentioning at this point that Darwin had with him aboard the *Beagle* a copy of Alexander von Humboldt's *Personal Narrative of Travels to the Equinoctial Regions of a New Continent*, 1799–1804, inscribed as follows: 'J. S. Henslow to his friend C. Darwin, on his departure from England upon a voyage round the World, 21 September 1831'.
3. Many of the specimens he sent back to Professor Henslow.
4. The bulk of these manuscripts are now held in the Manuscripts Room, Cambridge University Library, having been placed there by the Darwin family in 1942. The *Beagle* papers are mainly in folios designated DAR 29–42. They are apparently in the order in which they were left on Charles Darwin's death in 1882.
5. These are held at Down House, Downe, Kent, Darwin's home from 1841 until his death in April 1882, and of members of his family until the turn of the century. Down House is now the Charles Darwin Memorial.
6. Cambridge University Library Manuscripts (CULM) DAR 38.1/858. It is dated 'Tuesday'. The only Tuesday that the *Beagle* was at King George's Sound was 8 March 1836; quite possibly they were written up the day the observations were made.
7. These pencil notes are apparently dated '9th', presumably Wednesday 9 March 1836. The roughly written-up account of one day's observations seems thus to have been used as a note-pad the following day!
8. Captain FitzRoy in his account: *Narrative of the Surveying Voyages of His Majesty's Ships* Adventure *and* Beagle, 1826–1836 ..., Henry Colburn, London, 1839, noted:
   > Considering the limited disposable space in so very small a ship, we contrived to carry more instruments and books than one could readily suppose could be stored away in dry and secure places; and in a part of my own cabin twenty-two chronometers were carefully placed.
9. This was originally published, after a delay occasioned by Captain FitzRoy's illness, in 1839, as the final section of the *Narrative* (see Footnote 8); FitzRoy and Darwin's accounts complement one another admirably. No further very substantial alterations were made in preparing the 1845, 1860 or subsequent editions, although the second (1845) printing is described as 'corrected with additions' and the 1860 version is titled *A Naturalist's Voyage*. H. Gruber would argue that these corrections and additions are very significant for whereas the 1839 edition had been largely typeset (or at least was ready for the

74

press) by the time of Darwin's insight on the transmutability of species (probably in March 1837), the 1845 version was subtly evolutionary in places. See H. Gruber 'The Many Voyages of the *Beagle*', Appendix to 2nd edition of *Darwin on Man*.

10. The full original *Journal* was published, with the title *Charles Darwin's Diary of the Voyage of the Beagle*, edited by Nora Barlow, by Cambridge University Press in 1933. Mrs Barlow expressed the view that some of the marginal notes in the manuscript *Journal* were in the hand of Captain FitzRoy.
11. CULM/DAR 29.3/8.
12. CULM/DAR 29.1/17. *List of Fish in Spirits of Wine*. In Captain FitzRoy's account (*Narrative*, see footnote 8, p. 73) it is noted (p. 628) that 'twenty different kinds' of fish were caught, and that a seine net was used.
13. *Zoology of the Voyage of H.M.S. Beagle*, 1832-1836, published with the approval of the Lords Commissioners of Her Majesty's Treasury, edited by Charles Darwin, London, Smith Elder and Co., 1842. Part I, *Fossil Mammalia*, by Richard Owen; Part II, *Living Mammalia*, by George R. Waterhouse; Part III, *Birds*, by John Gould; Part IV, *Fish*, by Leonard Jenyns; Part V, *Reptiles*, by Thomas Bell.
14. CULM/DAR 29.1/36.
15. CULM/DAR 29.3/8.
16. CULM/DAR 29.3/78.
17. *Manual of Geology*, by Charles Darwin. (Extracted from the *Admiralty Manual of Scientific Enquiry*, Third Edition, 1859.)
18. Sulloway makes quite a point of Darwin's deficiencies in collecting, particularly in respect to birds and tortoises from the Galapagos Is. For example, he 'mingled together' (Darwin's phrase) bird specimens from several of the islands, beclouding their evolutionary significance, and the difficulties this caused was only partly resolved by his collaboration with the ornithologist John Gould. Further he quite literally let vital evidence in the form of Galapagos tortoises 'slip through his fingers', for several dozen tortoises were taken on board H.M.S. *Beagle* as food, eaten, and the bones thrown overboard! See F. J. Sulloway (1982) Darwin's Conversion: The *Beagle* Voyage and its Aftermath. *Journal of the History of Biology*, 15, pp. 325-96.
19. Besides the *Voyage of the Beagle* (footnote 9), and the *Zoology of the Voyage* (footnote 13), which he edited in collaboration with Jenyns, Waterhouse and Owen, Charles Darwin wrote the *Geology of the Voyage of the Beagle*, in three volumes: *The Structure and Distribution of Coral Reefs* (London, 1842); *Geological Observations on the Volcanic Islands Visited on the Voyage of H.M.S. Beagle* (London, 1844); and *Geological Observations on South America* (London, 1846).
20. CULM/DAR 29.1.
21. CULM/DAR 29.1/36.
22. Darwin's letters have been published in: *The Life and Letters of Charles Darwin* edited by his son Francis Darwin, three volumes, John Murray, London, 1903; *Darwin and Henslow: the Birth of an Idea* (footnote 2). The 'Family' *Beagle* letters were obviously particularly valued by the family and bound into a handsome folio sometime in the nineteenth century. CULM/DAR 223, on deposit from Down House.

23. See footnote 8.
24. *Narrative*, Volume 2, page 33.
25. CULM/DAR 41/1-21
26. Some editions have February 7th; this is a misprint.
27. *Narrative*, page 624.
28. *Narrative*, page 625. The expression 'Next day, however, we found that' at the commencement of the paragraph describing Sir Richard's farm, in Fitz-Roy's account serves to fix the date of the visit, and confirms that he was accompanied by Darwin.
29. A good account of the history of the property is found in M. Lukis, *The Old Farm, Strawberry Hill*, published by the National Trust of Australia (W.A.), undated. Many of the documents relating to the history of the farm are held in the muniment room at Strawberry Hill. These include a pencil sketch of the area, showing enclosed, cultivated ground drawn by H. M. Ommaney in 1836.
30. Friction with Aborigines over their traditional burning of bushland, killing of domestic animals, and other matters, was not unusual in the early days of settlement at King George's Sound, the Swan River, and of course, elsewhere in Australia. Yet many early European explorers, settlers and administrators worked hard to maintain good relations with the Aboriginal community. See D. A. P. West, *The Settlement of the Sound*, W.A. Museum, Perth, 1976; S. Hallam, *Fire and Hearth*, Australian Institute of Aboriginal Studies, Canberra, 1975; P. H. Armstrong, Aboriginal firing of the bush: the evidence of early newspapers, *Transactions at the Royal West Australian Historical Society*, Vol. 8(3), pages 31-4, 1978.
31. CULM/DAR 38.1/858; see also page 6 for comments on the absence of notebooks for south-west Australia.
32. He stresses this in all accounts of the excursion: in his preliminary notes, the *Geological Diary*, the *Journal*, the published *Voyage*, and his more specialised *Geological Observations of Volcanic Islands*.
33. CULM/DAR 38.1/867-68.
34. It is worth remembering that Captain FitzRoy was a competent scientist in his own right: he seems to have had some knowledge of geology. Charles' copy of Lyell's *Principles of Geology*, Volume I is inscribed 'Given by Captain R. Fitz-Roy'.
35. In a footnote Darwin comments: 'These and all other references are at present entirely drawn from Dr Fritton's appendix to King's Australia', see Appendix page 69.
36. See Geological Survey of Western Australia, *Mt. Barker-Albany* 1:250,000, Sl 50 – 11/15, preliminary edition, 1982. Quartz-feldspar-biotite gneiss, augen gneiss, porphyritic granite and dolerite all outcrop in close juxtaposition in this area.
37. CULM/DAR 38.1/865-66.
38. Possibly Middleton Beach.
39. *Zoological Diary*, CULM/DAR 31.2/349. The account is headed: Coast of Australia. For notes on the probable nature of the organisms I am indebted to Mr Barry David Scott, Royal Australian Navy Research Laboratory, Darlinghurst, N.S.W.

40. These are now held with the Darwin Archives at Cambridge University Library, but are as yet unclassified. They were formerly held by the Cambridge University Department of Earth Sciences, where Darwin's rock specimens are retained.
41. CULM/DAR 31.2/349.
42. This is not to say that earlier naturalists had ignored behaviour. Some (such as Gilbert White) had made the observation of animal behaviour an important part of their responsibilities. Darwin probably took seriously Henslow's enjoinder, given in his letter of 24 August 1831, that he was 'amply qualified for collecting, observing and noting anything worthy to be noted in Natural History', Letter No. 3, *Darwin and Henslow* (footnote 2). But Animal Behaviour was not regarded as an organised branch of science for many decades.
43. Now called the Cocos Islands, and an Australian External Territory, but having close links with Western Australia.
44. CULM/DAR 31.2/362 note on specimen 1428.
45. i.e. Mauritius.
46. Bob Keenan (Pace University, New York) has suggested to me two further aspects of Darwin's comparative approach in his 'pre-evolutionary insight' days. In some cases the descriptions are comparisons of a novel species with a familiar British form, ultimately this formed a useful way of communicating his discoveries to the British scientific community. Second the linking of the novel to the familiar constituted and aid to his own memory.
47. See note 2, page 73.
48. A reference, presumably, to exfoliation of the granite.
49. CULM/DAR 38.1/864. Again note Darwin's careful comparison with other environments, on the basis of published sources, and . . .
50. . . . his own experiences elsewhere.
51. If one dates the 'effectual colonization' from the arrival of Sir Richard Spencer as Government Resident in September 1833 (see p. 15), this is absolutely accurate.
52. CULM/DAR 38.1/867.
53. See footnote 35.
54. *Volcanic Islands*, 1838, page 149.
55. CULM/DAR 38.1/868-81.
56. CULM/DAR 38.1/868-81.
57. In his one-paragraph summary of his description of the site of *The Voyage of the Beagle*, Darwin refers to 'the place mentioned by so many navigators'.
58. CULM/DAR 38.1/875-78.
59. CULM/DAR 38.1/879.
60. V. Semeniuk and T.D. Meagher, Calcrete in Quaternary coastal dunes in southwestern Australia: a capillary-rise phenomenon associated with plants. *Journal of Sedimentary Petrology*, Vol. 51(1), pp. 47-67 (1981).
61. Semeniuk and Meagher, 1981, see footnote 60.
62. In his sister's letter of 12 February 1836, although she expressed delight at his 'fame and glory' and success in the world of science, she laments 'I fear there are but small hopes of your still going into the Church.' (CULM/DAR 97.30-31).

63. For a full exposition of these ideas and their relevance to Darwin's thinking, see Dov Ospovat, *The Development of Darwin's Theory: Natural History, Natural Theology, Natural Selection, 1838-1859*, Cambridge University Press, 1981, and more briefly, Howard Gruber and Paul Barrett, *Darwin on Man*, London, Wildwood House, 1974.
64. Albeit a creationist of an unusual kind, for he had by then absorbed the doctrines of uniformitarian geology — see page 52.
65. *Darwin and Henslow* (footnote 2), Letter 41, 9 July 1836.
66. See note 63.
67. Assuming F. J. Sulloway's date of March 1837 for 'Darwin's Final Conversion' is accepted (see footnote 18).
68. On certain areas of elevation and subsidence in the Pacific and Indian Oceans as deduced from the study of coral formations. *Proceedings of the Geological Society of London*, 2, 552-54, 1837. Reprinted in Paul H. Barrett, *The Collected Papers of Charles Darwin*, Vol. 1, University of Chicago Press, 1977, pp. 46-9.
69. At the foot of CULM/DAR 38.1/863.
70. Compare the quotations from the coral paper (p. 55) and the letter (p. 54).
71. C. Darwin, 1837: Observations of proofs of recent elevation on the coast of Chili, made during the survey of His Majesty's Ship *Beagle*, commanded by Captain FitzRoy, RN., *Proc. Geol. Soc. London*, 2, pp. 446-9.
72. *Proceedings of the Geological Society*, see footnote 68.
73. See page 49. Darwin's work on Bald Head may thus be seen to stand between his work on the terraces of Coquimbo and his 'Observations on the Parallel Roads of Glen Roy' in Scotland (*Phil. Trans. Royal Society*, 1839, pp. 39-81), where he similarly asserted (also erroneously) that the terraces were marine and caused by elevation of the shoreline. He later conceded that in the Glen Roy case he had made 'a gigantic blunder; and that every word of the Glen Roy paper is false. See especially: M. Rudwick (1974): 'Darwin and Glen Roy: A "Great Failure" in scientific method', *Studies Hist. Philos. Science* 5, pp. 97-185.
74. See page 12.
75. See footnote 13.
76. William Clift, of the College of Surgeons, London. In regard to the fossil bones found in the caves and bone breccia of New Holland. *Edinburgh New Philosophical Journal*, (1830-1831), pp. 394-96.
77. Published in *Evolution by Natural Selection: Papers by Charles Darwin and Alfred Russel Wallace*, Edited by Sir Gavin de Beer, Cambridge University Press, 1958. See pages 203-4.
78. *Ibid.* (footnote 77), p. 8.
79. Sulloway (footnote 18) has emphasised just how much of this occurred to Darwin *after* his visit. It must not be assumed that the full insight occurred actually during his stay on the islands.
80. Emma's Recipe Book (CULM, unclassified) contains a recipe for Compote of Apples, marked 'Dr Hooker, June 1844'.
81. D. M. Churchill, 1961. The tertiary and quaternary vegetation and climate in relation to the living flora of southwestern Australia. *Ph.D. thesis*, University of Western Australia.

82. *The Red Notebook of Charles Darwin*, edited by Sandra Herbert. 1980 British Museum (Natural History) and Cornell University Press; London and Ithaca.
83. Later Herschel was not sympathetic to Darwin's ideas. For a general review of Herschel's influence on Darwin, see M. Ruse, 1975; Darwin's debt to philosophy: an examination of the influences of the philosophical ideas of John F. W. Herschel and William Whewell on the development of Charles Darwin's theory of evolution, *Studies in History and Philosophy of Science* 6, pp. 159–81.

INDEX

Aborigines, 13, 17-20, 36, 38, 40, 75
Allan, Mea, 3

Babington, Charles, 4, 11, 12
Bald Head, 7, 8, 19, 22, 23, 30, 43, 44, 45-9, 55, 56, 57, 71, 77
Barlow, Nora, 6, 73
Bathurst, NSW, 4
Beagle, H.M.S., 1, 3, 4, 6, 8, 9, 10, 11, 12, 13, 14, 15, 17, 19, 22, 23, 27, 29, 30, 35, 38, 39, 46, 52, 53, 57, 58, 62, 65, 67, 68, 71, 73, 74, 77
Beagle Record, The, 3
blackboys (grass-trees), 3, 19, 35, 36, 37, 61
Butler, Rev. Samuel, 3

Cape Leeuwin, 28, 29
Cape of Good Hope, 30, 41, 71-2
Cape Verde Islands, 4
Casuarina, 35, 61
Charles Darwin and the Beagle, 6
Christ's College, Cambridge, 4, 51
cockatoos, 59
Cockatoo tribe, 17-20
Cocos-Keeling Islands, 8, 13, 14, 29, 30, 31, 32, 54, 55, 56, 70, 76
confervae: *see* phytoplankton
convicts, 38
coral atoll theory, 50, 52-3, 55, 56, 58, 65, 74, 77
corroboree, 17-20, 36, 38
crabs, 31-2

Dampier, William, 69-70
Darwin and Huxley in Australia, 3
Darwin and his Flowers, 3
Darwin College, Cambridge, 1
Darwin, Caroline, 39, 54
Darwin, Charles, Sir (1887-1962), 1
Darwin, Elizabeth (née Hill), 1
Darwin, Emma (née Wedgwood), 1, 63, 64, 77
Darwin, Erasmus, 71

Darwin, Francis, 74
Darwin, Robert, Dr, 4
Darwin, William Alvey, 1
D'Entrecasteaux, 22
Descent of Man, 3
diaries, 4, 6, 7, 8, 9, 11, 22, 24, 25, 31, 35, 42, 45, 55, 68, 69, 70, 74, 75
Down House, Kent, 10, 63, 73, 74
D'Urville, Dumont, 19
dyke, dike, 8, 22, 23, 26, 42, 43, 45, 69

Edinburgh, 4
emu, 59
emu dance, 18
Essay of 1844, 9, 60, 62-3, 65
eucalypts, 35, 59, 61

Falkland Islands, 4
feldspar, 22, 34, 43
fish, 9, 27, 38, 59, 74
Fitzroy, Captain, 6, 7, 9, 10, 13, 14, 15, 16, 17, 18, 20, 22, 23, 26, 29, 38, 40, 44, 47, 57, 69, 73, 74, 75, 77
Flinders, Captain, 10, 13, 22, 23, 70
Flinders Peninsula, 23, 49
fossils, 4, 8, 10, 30, 41, 47-9, 57, 77
Freycinet, 23

Galapagos Islands, 4, 11, 30, 52, 53, 54, 60-1, 64, 65, 71, 74
geological observations, 6, 20-6, 33-6, 41-9, 50, 56, 62, 68-9
gneiss, 23, 26, 35, 68, 75
granite, 22, 26, 34, 35, 36, 42, 43, 45, 46, 49, 68, 69, 70, 75, 76
grass-trees: *see* blackboys
Great Australian Bight, 4
Gruber, Howard, 50, 53, 57, 73, 74, 77

Helix, 23, 47
Henslow, Rev. Professor John Stevens, 4, 10, 11, 12, 39, 51, 52, 59, 64, 65, 68, 69, 73, 74, 75, 76, 77

Herbert, Mrs Sandra, 67, 68, 78
Herschel, Sir John, 71-2, 78
Hobart, 4, 13, 14, 30, 39
Hooker, Dr Joseph, 62-3, 64, 65, 71, 77
Hope, F. W., 11
Humboldt, Alexander von, 10, 35
hydrographic charts, 13

insects, 4, 11, 12, 52, 59
Indian Ocean, 13, 29, 56, 58, 77

Jenyns, Rev. Leonard, 9, 59, 65, 74

kangaroos, 18, 20, 27, 59
Keeling Islands: *see* Cocos-Keeling Islands
Kennedy, B. H., 3
Keynes, R. D., 3
King, Captain Phillip Parker, 10, 13, 22, 46, 69, 75
King George's Sound, 1, 3, 4, 6, 8, 11, 12, 13, 14, 15, 17, 19, 20, 21, 22, 27, 29, 30, 33, 35, 36, 39, 40, 41, 48, 51, 55, 56, 57, 61, 64, 68, 69, 70, 75

Labillardière, 11, 68, 70
Lake Seppings, 23, 27
Limestone Head, 23, 49
Lyrell, Charles, 10, 50, 52, 53-7, 58, 61, 62, 65, 71, 72, 75

magnetic observations, 13, 15, 26
mammals, 4, 9, 10, 12, 59, 60, 61, 74
Mauritius, 13, 14, 30, 31, 39, 65, 76
Michaelmas Island, 23, 49, 70
Middleton Beach, 23, 27
Mistaken Isle, 23, 42, 49

National Trust of Western Australia, 16, 75
natural theology, 51, 77
Newnham, 1
New South Wales, 4, 30, 36, 38, 39, 51-2, 59, 61
New Zealand, 4, 6, 30, 41, 62
Notebook, The Red, 9, 11, 67-72, 78
notebooks, 6, 7, 9, 11-12, 22, 30, 55, 60, 61, 65, 67, 75

Origin of Species, 3, 9, 53, 60, 62, 67
Oniscus, 23, 47
Oyster Bay, 22, 23

Pacific Ocean, 4, 50, 52-5, 56, 58, 77
petrified trees, 22, 47-9
phytoplankton (confervae), 28-9, 30-1, 68, 75

Port Jackson (Sydney), NSW, 4, 8, 13, 14, 39
plants, 3, 4, 8, 22, 27, 31, 35, 47-9, 51, 53, 55, 58, 59, 61-2, 63, 64, 77
Princess Royal Harbour, 9, 14, 15, 23, 26, 43, 49
Principles of Geology, 10, 50, 52-7, 58, 61-2, 71-2, 75

quartz, 22, 34, 35, 45, 70, 75

Raverat, Gwen, 1
reptiles, 4, 12, 74
rhizoconcretions, 44, 45, 47-9
rock specimens, 4, 10, 30, 41, 76

St Helena, 52, 65
St John's College, Cambridge, 12
St Paul's Rocks, 4

Sedgwick, Rev. Professor Adam, 4, 41
sedimentary rocks, 44-6, 48, 55, 64, 69, 70
shells, 8, 27, 47, 59
Shrewsbury, 3, 11, 30, 51, 73
Sketch of 1842, 9, 60, 62
South America, 4, 11, 12, 35, 36, 41, 42, 50, 52, 56, 59, 68, 77
specimen collecting, 4, 10, 12, 27, 31, 59, 74
Spencer, Sir Richard, 15-16, 75, 76
Strawberry Hill Farm, 15, 16, 75
Sullivan, Lt. Bartholomew, 15, 26
Swan River, 13, 14, 36, 64, 75
Sydney: *see* Port Jackson, NSW

Tahiti, 4, 52-3, 56
Tasmania, 4, 6, 14, 59, 61, 62, 63, 64, 65
Torres Strait, 13
transmutability of species, 11, 50, 54-5, 58, 60, 61, 63, 64, 65, 67, 71-2, 74

Vancouver, Captain, 22
Vancouver Peninsula, 19, 22, 23
Van Diemen's Land, 4, 6, 11, 14, 41; *see also* Tasmania
veins, 22, 42, 43, 69
Voyage of the Beagle, The, 7, 8, 9, 13, 14, 27, 36, 40, 57, 59, 61, 62, 65, 74, 75, 76

Wales, 4, 16, 68
Waterhouse, George, 12, 59, 74
Wedgwood, Josiah, 4

Zoonomia, 71